University of Washington Publications in History

The American Law of Treason

REVOLUTIONARY

AND EARLY NATIONAL ORIGINS

BRADLEY CHAPIN

UNIVERSITY OF WASHINGTON PRESS

SEATTLE

To Bink and Midge

Acknowledgments

Though the book is brief, the list of my creditors is substantial. Three professors—Julius W. Pratt and John T. Horton of the State University of New York at Buffalo, and Curtis P. Nettels of Cornell University—helped me as I wrote various parts of the manuscript. I am particularly indebted to Mr. Nettels. Of my colleagues at Cornell a decade ago, Allen J. McCurry and James M. Smith worked in related fields and helped me much in the process.

The archivists and librarians of a number of states and societies helped me either in person or through correspondence. I wish to thank them for permission to use, and in many cases make copies of, manuscripts in their possession. The depositories used in person or by agent were: the Public Record Office, London; the Library of Congress; the state libraries of New Jersey and New York; the Historical Society of Pennsylvania; the New York Historical Society; the Hall of Records at Annapolis; the New York Public Library. The documents in the Public Record Office were read by a London barrister, Robert Stevens. In addition, I corresponded with or visited county depositories in several states. These excursions demonstrated how harshly time has dealt with many of our early legal records.

Two chapters appeared in slightly different form in the *William and Mary Quarterly* and the *Pennsylvania Magazine of History and Biography*. I am indebted to the editors of those journals, Lawrence W. Towner and Nicholas B.

Wainwright, not only for permission to reprint, but also for helpful comments.

One other author, Willard B. Hurst, has written on the subject of the early American law of treason. His study has been published in the *Harvard Law Review* and as an appendix to the brief in the case of *Anthony Cramer v. the United States*. Hurst's work is especially valuable for its analysis of the constitutional and statutory materials.

Finally, my thanks to Nancy who has helped with the mechanics of this book while raising a numerous brood.

BRADLEY CHAPIN

Buffalo, New York
August, 1963

Contents

The American Law of Treason

1

English and Colonial Background

The constitutional definition of treason against the United States, a substantial example of eighteenth-century liberal statesmanship,[1] is cast precisely in the words of a fourteenth-century English statute. By what process did the medieval become modern, the monarchical republican? The roots of our substantive law are in a statute of Edward III.[2] Of the seven heads of action made treasonable by the ancient law, the more significant were: compassing or imagining the death of the king, adhering to the king's enemies, giving them aid and comfort, and levying war against the king. For several centuries after 1351, Parliament expanded or contracted the treason law by statute, in most cases temporarily. Continuing threats to the monarchs of the Reformation period showed modification of the law by legislative action to be unsatisfactory. In Elizabeth's time crown lawyers began constructing new treasons by expanding the meaning of the statute of Edward III. Gradually the old statute lost its restrictive influence. Of these judicially constructed treasons, the most important were that words, spoken or written, and conspiracies to levy war could amount to the treason of compassing or imagining the death of the king, and that any attempt to modify public policy by force amounted to treason. Under the latter doctrine any attempt to prevent the application of a statute was not riot, but treason.[3]

Stuart judges often used these constructive treasons to

stamp out resistance, particularly after the Restoration. They pushed to extremes the doctrine that words were sufficiently overt acts to prove an intent to compass the king's death. The publication of a tract which suggested that the king was accountable to the people brought a treason conviction in 1663.[4] Jeffrey gave the doctrine of treasonable words ultimate expression in the celebrated case of Algernon Sydney; an unpublished manuscript proved to be Sydney's undoing.[5] The Stuart judges also used the expanded concept of levying war. Only the chief justice dissented when King's Bench ruled that the pulling down of bawdy houses was in fact an act of high treason.[6]

The revolution of 1688 brought changes in the procedural aspects of the treason law. The Treason Trials Act of 1696 guaranteed a fair trial by providing, *inter alia*, that no person could be convicted of treason except on the testimony of two witnesses to the same overt act; that the accused should have a copy of the indictment and the list of the jury panel before trial; that process of the court should be made available to compel witnesses to attend in behalf of the defense.[7]

The upsetting of the Stuart monarchy brought no reform to the substantive law, although it created the necessity for a dual theory of resistance, one political, one legal. In the realm of politics, the great majority of Englishmen accepted the theory of resistance that had produced the new constitutional settlement. John Locke's ideas on revolution became orthodox.[8] In the area of the criminal law, the older theories of resistance prevailed. The courts preferred the doctrines that had protected the Tudor and Stuart monarchs.

This dualism was illustrated with striking clarity in the affair of Dr. Henry Sacheverell.[9] In 1710, the doctor, an Anglican clergyman, preached and published two harangues in which he expanded upon his favorite theme of passive obedience and nonresistance. The Whig ministry brought charges of impeachment. The case gave everyone, including the Tories, a chance to go on record in favor of the principles of 1688. A Whig was distinguished from a Tory only by the speed with which he would theoretically draw the weapon of resistance.

While parliamentarians rang the changes on the glory of the late happy revolution, resistance took a more realistic form in the London streets. Many interpreted the impeachment of Sacheverell as an attack on the church. The doctor's denunciation of the Toleration Act helped set in motion a mob which pulled down several dissenting meeting houses. The government brought the leading rioters to trial, alleging a levying of war. In charging the jury, the chief justice stated the law precisely as his Stuart and Tudor predecessors had done.[10] At the same moment, in cases arising out of the same circumstances, resistance had been justified in Parliament but had been called treason by the courts. The constitution had changed, the criminal law had not.

The judicially constructed treasons remained alive through the eighteenth century. The passage of an effective riot act in 1715 made frequent use of the doctrine of constructed war unnecessary, but the law remained unchanged.[11] In 1781 the Earl of Mansfield, lord chief justice, stated the law as it had been understood for two centuries,[12] and in 1795 Parliament placed this area of the law on a statutory basis.[13] The judges also kept alive that part of the law accepting many overt acts as evidence of compassing the death of the king. In the 1690's, convictions were obtained on indictments alleging printing and conspiracy as acts showing an intent to compass the king's death.[14] From these substantive and procedural roots, an American law of treason grew.

Provincial criminal law bore little resemblance to the common law in the first period of colonization. The first statutes and codes defining treason used unfamiliar terms. The early legislators tended to use a similar vocabulary when they established as treason such crimes as mutiny, sedition, desertion, attempts to alter or subvert government, or raising "public Rebellion." In many cases, particularly in the Puritan colonies of New England, the definitions were Biblically inspired. In all cases, they reflect the fears felt by infant communities on a raw frontier of internal dissension and foreign invasion.[15]

By the last years of the seventeenth century the process of shaping Colonial law more closely after English models began. Several New England colonies copied or paraphrased closely the statute of Edward III. They also took over the procedural rules set out in the Trial of Treasons Act of 1696. A more common practice was to pass legislation that adopted the English substantive and procedural rules without setting out these rules in detail.[16]

In some areas, the Colonial legislatures extended the definition of treason beyond the boundaries of the English law. The French Wars caused colonies such as New York and Massachusetts to be concerned with what acts amounted to adhering to the enemy, giving him aid and comfort. The common law prescribed no clear rule as to whether trading with the enemy amounted to treason. The provincial assemblies regarded trading with the enemy sometimes as a misdemeanor, sometimes as treason. A Massachusetts statute of 1706 also declared "holding a traiterous [*sic*] correspondence" with the enemy to be treason.[17] On occasion, special local circumstances caused Colonial legislatures to modify or extend the law. For example, in the 1680's Virginians attempted to control tobacco prices by destroying young plants. As a result of the great disorder, the legislature defined such an act as not riot, but treason. The stormy New York politics of the 1690's produced another example. The execution of Jacob Leisler left a legacy of bitterness and hatred. In order to make future prosecution of political opponents a simple matter, the anti-Leislerian legislature passed a law making it treason "to disturb the peace and quiet" of the government "by force of arms or otherwise." This was the ultimate in a loose and dangerous law of treason.[18]

In practice, the great Colonial treason, levying war, took many forms. Such crimes fell into three categories: actual armed insurrection; war by construction (that is, aggravated resistance to the execution of law); and novel treasons that translated some act of political opposition into the high crime. The best examples of outright insurrection are Bacon's armed challenge of Berkeley[19] and the Regulators' resistance to Tryon at the Alamance.[20] Jacob Leisler's armed defense of Fort George in the face of royal troops, and his refusal to surrender to Governor Sloughter, amounted to levying war.[21] The attempt of the "Long Finn" to detach the Delaware settlement from the Duke of York's jurisdiction probably belongs in the category of bona fide insurrection.[22] The Virginia plant-cutters' rebellion is the best example of a constructive levying of war. Governor and council debated the question whether this misguided effort to control tobacco prices amounted to riot or treason. Governor Culpeper, arguing that the forcible and general effort to destroy the plants came within the rule of *Queen v. Bradshaw,* forced a treason prosecution.[23] The New York antirent riots of the 1760's ended in brief, futile resistance to the Twenty-eighth Regiment. Though the leader of the rioters, William Prendergast, had directly levied war, the attorney general preferred to base the prosecution on the law of constructed war because the evidence relative to the antirent riots was much fuller.[24]

The novel Colonial treasons were used for various purposes. Sometimes such a charge facilitated the destruction of a defeated faction. New York brought Nicholas Bayard near the shadow of the gallows in an action based on a provincial statute that made any act of opposition to government levying war; the act alleged was the circulation of petitions critical of government.[25] In some cases, charges of treason were made to dramatize local grievances. A seventeenth-century grand jury indicted two men for high treason, alleging in one instance denial of trial by jury,[26] in another, collecting customs without proper authority.[27]

Procedurally, the record is a reasonable replica of English practice as established in the reported cases and the statute of 1696. Only the high courts, either the superior court or the circuit judge armed with the commissions of general gaol delivery and oyer and terminer, heard and determined cases of treason.[28] As in England, special commissions of oyer and terminer, fast and eclectic, were much used.[29] Of arrest and commitment, little is known. Indictments show a reasonably accurate imitation of English forms.[30] The plea on indictment was regular, and in one celebrated case the accused felt a modification of the *peine fort et dure* before being condemned as a "mute." [31] In defending himself, the accused traitor normally had the advantages guaranteed by the Trial of Treasons Act, though the statute was not in force in the Colonies: he had a list of the panel, a copy of the indictment, and counsel.[32] Judges accepted the statutory rules of evidence, requiring more than one witness to an overt act.[33] Judgment usually brought a motion to arrest, and, once given, carried the same inevitable consequence as judgment at King's Bench, attainder working a corruption of the blood and forfeiture.[34] In sentencing, the judge read the barbarous old formula calling for hanging, disembowelment, and quartering.[35] Normally the governor stayed execution, and often appeal to English authorities brought reversal of judgment.[36]

A survey of the law in action in several Colonial jurisdictions leads to these conclusions: the magistrates used the old law on an *ad hoc* basis, selecting the substantive and procedural rules necessary to meet local emergencies; no native body of American precedent emerged, but scrutiny of a century's intermittent experience discloses a bench and bar increasingly familiar with English case and statute. No frontier thesis, depicting a crude jurisprudence based largely on Coke's *Institutes,* will explain the first formative era in relation to this head of law.[37] In using the English law of treason, the colonists made small innovations, largely in relation to the substantive law. Eighteenth-century criminal law cried for reform, but to seek a process of rational clarification in the Colonial jurisdictions is fruitless. In 1775, the American law of treason was the law of England transferred to a new home. What was old far outweighed what was new.

2

The American Revolution

as Lese Majesty

British attempts after 1763 to force the American Colonies to conform to a renovated mercantile system called forth a vigorous opposition. Colonial and British views of the nature of this opposition were poles apart: the colonists saw themselves conducting a legal struggle for their constitutional rights; imperial servants regarded American action as criminal.

In 1763, crown attorneys had at their disposal a body of law which described aggravated riots, conspiracies to levy war, and verbal resistance as treason. The question inevitably came, would they make use of this law to break the back of American resistance?

Resistance to Grenville's new revenue policy first raised the issue of treason in America. New York newspapers united in outspoken criticism of the Stamp Act, and these "Scandalous and Treasonable" writings set government in motion. Cadwallader Colden immediately met his council, to which General Thomas Gage reported that he was greatly disturbed "to see the Public Papers crammed with Treason." [1] Early in November, 1765, opposition to the act passed from the stage of words to action. A great mob spilled into the streets on the night of October 31, returning the next night to threaten Fort George. The immediate crisis passed when the people agreed to permit the stamps to be stored in the City

Hall. Violence flared again in January when a second shipment of stamps was burned.[2] During the trouble a new governor, Sir Harry Moore, arrived in New York. He showed a conciliatory attitude until new instructions from London underlined the point that the resistance was criminal and awakened him to the fact that duty demanded repression and punishment. Moore advised the council to suppress the treasonable gazettes and to ask Gage for a force to maintain order.[3]

Neither Colden, nor Gage, nor Moore could get any action from the council. The councilors stalled, procrastinated, and in the end did nothing.[4] The inaction of the New York council in the opening scene of the decade of crisis revealed one reason why the English law of treason could not be applied effectively. The agencies of provincial government would not regard as criminal the resistance that coincided with Colonial self-interest. The New York oligarchy that dominated the council had been implicated deeply in the opposition to the Stamp Act.[5] The notoriously ill-defined law of treason might easily have involved persons in embarrassingly high places, an event to be avoided at all costs.[6]

One thing is certain: the council had no prejudice against treason proceedings as such. While the city rocked with the Stamp Act controversy, the back country flamed into open revolt as rioters on the great Dutchess estates rose against their landlords. The council repressed this discontent, which threatened their control of the internal economy, with sudden severity. A special commission of oyer and terminer moved in behind the Twenty-eighth Regiment to try and to convict the rioters' leader of the treason of levying war.[7]

Once made public, the idea that Colonial resistance amounted to treason never died. Through 1766, Englishmen often referred to American action as "treasonable." A resolution passed along with the Declaratory Act described the activities in America as "tumults and insurrections."[8] In the debate, the lord chancellor noted that the legislature should make laws to promote the common good, but if the legislature violated its trust, the subject still owed obedience to the law. Opposition to law, even bad law, he said, was "at the risk of life and fortune." [9] In the same debate, a member of the Lords expressed the opinion that pamphlets like those written by James Otis had in the past "led the people to rebellion." [10] The distinction between internal and external taxes was described as "criminal and treasonable," [11] while some regarded John Dickinson's *Letters from a Farmer in Pennsylvania* as "treasonable and seditious." [12] Shelburne thought that the province of New York, by refusing to meet the requisition demanded by the Quartering Act, would be likely "in the talk of the town, to undergo the imputation of rebellion." [13] But these random and scattered examples reflect opinion only, not public policy.

The British policy in regard to American resistance began to develop in 1767. The reaction of Massachusetts to the Townshend duties and the remodeling of the customs service [14] brought the issue of Colonial treason to the attention of high officials in England. Early in November, 1767, the newly appointed commissioners of customs landed in Boston. They soon applied for naval assistance, and the *Romney* was stationed at Boston. On February 11, 1768, the lower house of the Massachusetts Legislature drew up a circular letter which invited other Colonial assemblies to examine the constitutionality of the late acts of Parliament and to petition for redress of grievance.[15] Refusal to rescind the circular letter resulted in the dissolution of the Assembly on June 31, 1768.[16] An attempt to collect the duty on wine imported in John Hancock's sloop *Liberty* had led to a riot on June 10, 1768. Early in August, the Boston merchants entered into a nonimportation agreement.[17] On September 22, the selectmen of Boston sent a circular letter to the towns, inviting them to attend a convention. After several desultory exchanges with Governor Francis Bernard, the convention drew up a document reciting their grievances.[18] On September 28, the first regiments that were to garrison Boston arrived from Halifax.

It is no longer possible to locate exactly the origins of the idea that the series of events described above was treason. The commissioners of the customs and Bernard described these actions in highly colored terms when they wrote to English officials.[19] By midsummer of 1768, high officers of the government were investigating the feasibility of treason trials.[20] Aware that local juries would be sympathetic to an accused traitor, they searched for a means of bringing persons suspected of treason to England. The ministry discovered an old statute passed in the reign of Henry VIII. This "act for the trial of treasons committed out of the King's dominions" had made possible the transportation of Irish traitors by providing that any treason committed out of the realm of England might be tried at Westminster before King's Bench or in any English county by special commissioners appointed by the king.[21]

The idea that the dramatic trial and execution of the leaders of Colonial resistance would restore order took root. In September, 1768, Secretary at War William Barrington wrote to Bernard expressing the hope that Boston would be quiet. He thought, however, that no pacification would be possible "unless some legal examples be made of persons concern'd in the late violences committed there." [22] Early in November, a few weeks before Parliament reconvened, the American secretary, the Viscount Hillsborough, sought the advice of the king's law officers. He sent papers describing affairs in Boston to the attorney general and the solicitor general, William DeGrey and John Dunning, asking them if these actions were criminal. The lawyers replied that the trials of Americans in England had to be based on 35 Henry

VIII, c. 2. This statute, however, applied only to treason, and they gave their opinion that the actions described in the papers did not amount to treason.[23]

Rebuffed by the law officers, the ministry turned to Parliament. In opening the second session of the thirteenth Parliament, George III announced from the throne that Massachusetts had proceeded "even to acts of violence, and of resistance to the execution of the law." Boston appeared "to be in a state of disobedience to all law and government." [24] Hillsborough then read extracts from the American papers to the Lords and moved eight resolves condemning the activities in Boston.[25] Immediately, the Duke of Bedford was on his feet reading an address to the king which assured him that Parliament would stand squarely behind any measures he wished to pursue in America. The address advised the king to make examples of those who had fomented disorder and requested him to instruct Bernard to obtain and transmit to England all information concerning treason or misprision of treason. The ministry desired the governor to send the names of the principal offenders to England so that they might be tried before a special commission as authorized in the statute 35 Henry VIII. The Lords approved the resolutions and address and sent them to the lower house.[26] In Commons the opposition members spoke their piece: the policy recommended by the address, they argued, denied the fundamental right of trial by a jury of the vicinage; it established dual standards of justice, one for Englishmen within the realm, another for those in the Colonies. Such a policy would permit a Colonial governor to "work off personal and political prejudices." The opposition attacked the statute of Henry VIII and the attempt to drag it out of oblivion, but their argument fell on deaf ears as the resolves and address passed, 169 to 65.[27]

The question remains, why did the ministry propose and pass the Bedford Address, knowing as they did that the law officers did not consider the activities in Boston to be treason? The opposition in Commons came close to the truth when they said that the policy could not be executed and, further, that the ministry had no intention of executing it.[28] The supporters of the address showed this to be true when they defended it as a preventive measure and a warning. They "were in hopes that such a seasonable shew of so much vigour and lenity, would operate to bring the people of the colonies to a sense of their duty." [29]

Reactions in America to the ministerial policy were mixed. Gage, who had earlier announced that he considered the action in Boston "a direct rebellion," [30] expressed disappointment. He informed Barrington that the Bedford Address had surprised many persons who had expected positive orders for the arrest and transportation of the leaders. He thought it ridiculous to expect more conclusive proof from Bernard, for, in the general's opinion, the available evidence was prima-facie proof of the Bostonians' guilt.[31] Bernard began to comply with the decrees of the ministry as expressed in the Bedford Address. He gathered evidence against individuals and sent it to England, but refused to go further than this.[32] In February, Barrington suggested that Bernard bring leaders to trial: "Five or Six Examples are sufficient; And it is right they should be made in Boston, the Only place where there has been actual Crime." [33] Bernard knew that such a policy could not be carried out. In a letter to Barrington he expressed the opinion that the policy of the Bedford Address could not be executed unless the home government armed him "with some extraordinary Power." [34]

The colonists, who had long striven to maintain local control of all judicial processes, saw at once the great threat to American liberty in the statute of Henry VIII. The legislature of Virginia protested the attempt to revive the statute as a departure from "the ancient and long established course of proceedings." [35] The Massachusetts Legislature resolved that all treasons committed in the colony should be tried in the provincial courts.[36] An American agent in London concluded: "If a perpetual & satisfactory settlement be intended . . . it appears strange that they should proceed to hang a rod over you, by searching after traitors in order to . . . their transportation and trial here, when there was no treason existing." [37]

Several years later, events in the colony of Rhode Island gave the ministry an opportunity to test the efficacy of the plan to bring suspected traitors to England for trial.

> Seventeen hundred and seventy-two,
> In Newport harbor lay a crew,
> That played the part of pirates there,
> The sons of freedom could not bear.

Fate intervened in the career of Lieutenant William Dudingston and the revenue schooner of which he was master, the *Gaspee.*

> Here, on the tenth day of last June,
> Betwixt the hours of twelve and one,
> Did chase the sloop, called the Hannah,
> Of whom, one Lindsay, was commander.
> They dogged her up Providence Sound,
> And there the rascal got around.
>
> .   .   .   .
>
> That night, about half after ten
> Some Narragansett Indian men,
> Being sixty-four, if I remember,
> Which made the stout coxcomb surrender;
> And what was best of all their tricks,
> They in his breech a ball did fix;
> Then set the men upon the land,
> And burnt her up, we understand.[38]

News of the destruction of the *Gaspee* set in motion the great engine of imperial administration. Hillsborough brought the affair to the attention of the cabinet, where the decision was made to ask the law officers for an opinion.[39] Dunning and DeGrey were gone, the former to the opposition benches in the Commons, the latter to serve North in the same place. They had been replaced by serviceable men, Edward Thurlow and Alexander Wedderburn. Hillsborough wrote to the lawyers, inquiring whether a statute regulating dockyards and ships applied to the Rhode Island affair; he wanted to know if the offenders could be brought to England for trial.[40] The law officers answered that the act to which the secretary had alluded applied only to ships in dockyards, but went on to say that the attack was "an Act of High Treason Vizt. of levying War against His Majesty." If the assault had taken place within some county in Rhode Island the offenders could be tried in the colony or be brought to England.[41]

On August 20, 1772, the cabinet decided to authorize special commissioners to investigate the affair.[42] The next day the Privy Council ordered the law officers to draft a commission and prepare a proclamation offering pardon to anyone who would act as informer.[43] The commission ordered three chief justices, Daniel Horsmanden of New York, Frederick Smyth of New Jersey, and Peter Oliver of Massachusetts, and a judge of vice-admiralty, Robert Auchmuty, to try to determine who had been involved in the destruction of the *Gaspee*. The proclamation offered £500 reward for the discovery of any persons concerned in the attack, and £1,000 for revealing who the leaders had been. Anyone implicated in the business who turned informer would receive full pardon and the reward. On August 26 the Privy Council ordered the documents to pass the Great Seal.[44]

As the council acted, the Earl of Dartmouth replaced Hillsborough as secretary of state for the colonies. Since the new secretary was not in London at the time, John Pownall wrote informing him that the affair of the *Gaspee* was of such great importance that he hoped the secretary would return to town before the dispatches were sent. Pownall wrote that the attorney general considered the affair as of "five times the magnitude of the Stamp Act." [45] Early in September, Dartmouth informed Governor Wanton of Rhode Island that a special commission had been appointed to help him get to the bottom of the crime. Under some circumstances, Dartmouth wrote, the action might have been regarded as piracy, but the law officers had given their opinion that the crime was "of a much deeper dye, and is considered in no other light, than as an act of high treason, viz.: levying war against the King." He instructed Wanton to turn over to Admiral John Montagu anyone apprehended so that he might be brought to England for trial.[46]

The commissioners sat at Newport early in 1773 and again in the spring of that year. Only one witness volunteered to accuse persons of implication in the affair, and his testimony was so confused as to be worthless.[47] All the power of the agencies of administration had been brought to bear on a limited object without result. The policy of removing suspected traitors to England for trial was a dismal failure. The *Gaspee* inquiry stands as testimony to Colonial solidarity. Even a large reward did not tempt the Rhode Islanders to expose those persons whose participation in the destruction of the *Gaspee* had gained local notoriety.[48]

> *Now, for to find these people out,*
> *King George has offered very stout;*
> *One thousand pounds to find out one*
> *That wounded William Dudingston.*
>
> .   .   .   .
>
> *One thousand more, there doth remain*
> *For to find out the leader's name;*
> *Likewise, five hundred pounds per man*
> *For anyone of all the clan.*

The American Revolution as Lese Majesty

But let him try his utmost skill,
I'm apt to think he never will
Find out any of those hearts of gold,
Though he should offer fifty fold.

After the Boston Tea Party in December, 1773, two main policies relative to treason in America are discernible. One of these policies had as its basis the assumption that responsibility for Colonial resistance could be fixed on individual leaders. The ministry might recommend the transportation of suspected traitors to England or direct imperial officers in the Colonies to begin proceedings in America. The second policy was of a different sort. The government would describe a political unit or geographic area—a city, colony, or group of colonies—as being in a state of rebellion in order to justify general coercive measures.

News of the destruction of the tea came to Dartmouth late in January, 1774. The cabinet again decided to ask the attorney and solicitor general for an opinion.[49] The law officers, applying rules of constructive treason, decided that the Bostonians had levied war against the king. Molineux, Denny, Warren, Williams, Church, Young, Hancock, Samuel Adams, the Boston committee of correspondence, the selectmen of the city, the town clerk, and members of the House of Representatives were named as possible traitors. These men might be arrested by local officials and tried in Boston, or be transported to England for trial upon a warrant issued by the secretary of state.[50]

On February 19, Dartmouth laid the American papers and the lawyers' opinion before the Privy Council. The councilors examined persons who had firsthand knowledge of the situation in Boston, but took no action.[51] By March 1, Thurlow and Wedderburn had reconsidered their opinion and retracted at least as much of it as applied to the transportation of suspects to England. The explanation of the change of opinion is to be found in a cabinet meeting held

19

sometime late in February. The ministers had their pens in hand ready to sign a warrant authorizing the transportation of specific persons. Two men waited outside Dartmouth's office and questioned Thurlow and Wedderburn as they left the meeting. Asked if the business had been accomplished, Thurlow replied:

No, nothing is done. Don't you see . . . that they want to throw the whole responsibility of the business upon the Solicitor General and me; and who would be such damned fools to risk themselves for such ———— fellows as these. No if it was George Grenville who was so damned obstinate that he would go to hell with you before he would desert you, there would be some sense in it.[52]

Another witness, John Pownall, said that Mansfield had prevented the signing of the warrant "by urging the other measures," presumably the Coercive Acts.[53] Mansfield himself said that the warrant had fallen through because Thurlow and Wedderburn reconsidered the evidence and concluded that it was insufficient to warrant transportation and trial.[54] North expressed a similar view.[55] Whatever the reason, the ministry abandoned the scheme temporarily.

The arrival in England of an obscure prisoner raised the hopes of the ministry in August, 1774. Gage had arrested Samuel Dyer for encouraging desertion among the king's troops. For a brief time, the ministry thought that Dyer would be able to give the evidence that would warrant the transportation of the Boston leaders. The expectation proved to be groundless because the lawyers were of the opinion that, since his testimony would not support a charge of treason, the statute of Henry VIII did not apply.[56]

Though the lawyers' specifications concerning evidence vitiated any attempt to apply the old statute, the threat of its application remained current for some months. The statute figured in parliamentary debate early in 1775, to be condemned as an attempt to "bring the Americans over

here to butcher them in the King's-bench." [57] The desire
to apply the statute to America was established sufficiently
to warrant defense in Samuel Johnson's pamphlet, *Taxation
No Tyranny*.[58]

The ministry continued to press attempts to try persons
in America. In April, 1774, Gage became governor of Massachusetts. Dartmouth enclosed the opinion of Thurlow and
Wedderburn that declared the Boston Tea Party to be an
act of treason. The secretary instructed General Gage to
make further inquiries. If the governor thought that it would
be possible to obtain a conviction on an indictment he
should begin proceedings.[59] In July, Gage reported his prog-
ress.[60] He had tried to gather evidence, "but tho' I hear of
many Things against this, and that Person, yet when I
descend to particular Points, and want People to stand forth
in order to bring Crimes home to Individuals by clear and
full Evidence, I am at a Loss." The ministry kept pressure
on Gage.[61]

When Dartmouth heard of the Suffolk Resolves and of
the opposition to the mandamus councilors, he again asked
Thurlow and Wedderburn for an opinion.[62] The lawyers
answered that acts of treason had been committed in Massachusetts.[63] Additional instructions went out to Gage in January, 1775—the "secret letter" that led to Lexington and
Concord.[64] Dartmouth thought that it would "surely be
better that the Conflict should be brought on [now] . . .
than in a riper state of Rebellion." As a corollary to military
action, the secretary advised the seizure and trial of prominent leaders. He enclosed the lawyers' opinion of December
13, 1774.[65]

Recent scholarship has discredited the idea that the
march of April 19 into the Massachusetts countryside had as
even a secondary objective the capture of Colonial leaders.
It has been pointed out that had Gage desired he could
easily have arrested leaders who remained in Boston.[66] This

may be true, but it is significant that Gage regarded his instructions on this point as sufficiently explicit to warrant an explanation of why he had not arrested John Hancock and Samuel Adams. Gage told Dartmouth that the "disaffected" received news of the ministerial action before he did. The leaders had fled just in time to escape the trap.[67] Adams and Hancock went in triumph to the Second Continental Congress instead of to prison. Their escape symbolized the attempts to bring men to trial in the Colonies. The ministerial policy failed as dismally as the efforts to transport men to England under the statute of Henry VIII.

But George III and his ministers were not to be denied easily. Yet another method of destroying the leaders of the resistance suggested itself during the winter of 1774–75. The ministry based its policy on the assumption that a few incendiaries were misleading the great mass of Americans. The idea became current that opposition could be quelled by offering a general pardon. The acts of the colonists would be described as treasonable, but at the same time pardon would be offered to all, except the leaders, who surrendered within a limited time and took an oath of allegiance. Threat of condign punishment would thus stop the growth of opposition, and the leaders would be left standing alone, to be dispatched with ease.

The cabinet first considered this idea in December, 1774.[68] Thurlow and Wedderburn put their stamp of approval on the plan and, by February, had drafted a proclamation.[69] The cabinet recommended that Gage be given the power to issue a proclamation pardoning the "rebels." Anyone who had attended the Massachusetts Provincial Congress or had been involved in the attack on Fort William and Mary would be ineligible for a pardon.[70] Dartmouth wrote to Gage in April, informing him that he might issue a proclamation.[71]

By the time Gage received Dartmouth's letter, Lexington and Concord had been fought and the general was besieged in Boston. General Gage issued his proclamation on June 12, 1775. The preamble stated the ministerial theory of the nature of Colonial opposition: ". . . the infatuated multitude, who have long suffered themselves to be conducted by certain well known incendiaries and traitors, in a fatal progression of crimes against the constitutional authority of the State, have at length proceeded to avowed Rebellion." [72] The document promised pardon to all who would lay down their arms, excepting only Samuel Adams and John Hancock. All who remained with the army around Boston, or who supplied that army, or corresponded with it, were proclaimed "to be Rebels and Traitors, and as such to be treated." The proclamation closed by declaring martial law.

Gage's proclamation signified the end and the failure of the attempt to bring individual leaders to trial. The subsequent growth of the spirit of American independence proved the error of the ministerial theory that the isolation of a few leaders, by declaring them to be traitors, would put a stop to Colonial opposition.

At the same time that it attempted to bring individuals to trial, the ministry unfolded a second plan of action—general coercive measures justified by charges of treason in America. Although none of the Coercive Acts directly branded the New Englanders as traitors, it was clear that only treason could justify such punitive measures. The Boston Port Act spoke of "dangerous commotions and insurrections," [73] while the Massachusetts Government Act described provincial leaders proceeding "even to acts of direct resistance to, and defiance of, His Majesty's authority." [74] Lord North knew that he was opening himself to criticism by using treason to justify his policy. Inevitably, the opposition would ask if there could be treason without traitors, and would demand the punishment of individuals before annihilating the rights of a whole colony. To avoid such criticism, North told the Commons that he ardently wished to see the ringleaders brought to justice and that the ministry had ordered prosecutions. His main defense of the Administration of Justice Act was that royal servants in America could not try individual traitors until the protection the act provided was extended to them.[75]

By the autumn of 1774, the idea that Massachusetts was in a state of rebellion had become common in ministerial circles.[76] The policy of coercion adopted earlier in the year had solidified American resistance, and the ministry expected further crises. Determined to press the issue, the king dissolved Parliament while it still had six months to run. The reason for the dissolution, according to North, was that the ministry "might, at the beginning of a Parliament take such measures as we could depend upon a Parliament to prosecute to effect." [77] In his speech opening the new Parliament, George III referred to the opposition in Massachusetts which had "broke forth in fresh violences of a very criminal nature." [78] Early in the session, Parliament debated the English merchants' petition for reconciliation with America, Chatham's provisional act for settling the American troubles, and his motion for withdrawing the troops from Boston. The overwhelming majorities that the ministry enjoyed in both houses drowned conciliation in a flood of contempt. The prevailing attitude found apt expression in the speech of young Lord Stanley, who "expatiated largely on the legislative supremacy and omnipotence of parliament; spoke much of treason, rebellion, coercion, and firmness." [79]

Early in February, 1775, North again put his political machine in motion. He brought in an address to the king on the American troubles and in the process of defending it named those Colonies in which there was a "state of actual rebellion." Mansfield, North's counterpart in the upper house, carried the address in the Lords by legal argument proving that the Colonies were in a state of rebellion. The address, which declared that "a rebellion actually exists" in Massachusetts, urged the king to adopt a rigorous policy. It passed by large majorities.[80] Having created the fiction of parliamentary initiative, North brought in the New England Restraining Bill.[81] He justified the bill on the ground that Massachusetts was in rebellion. The system of coercion was now to be extended to all New England, for New Hampshire had caught the treason fever and seized Fort William and Mary.[82] Dunning, by this time one of the tiny minority who spoke for Colonial liberty, accused the ministry of creating the rebellion. Thurlow answered by stating again that the common law upheld the contention that rebellion existed in New England.[83] Parliament passed the bill and followed it with one interdicting the commerce of the southern Colonies.[84]

As yet the ministry had used treason in America only to justify coercive measures and had stopped short of branding the Americans as rebels by any public act. In August, 1775, a royal Proclamation of Rebellion declared that the North American Colonies had "proceeded to open and avowed rebellion, by arraying themselves in a hostile manner, to withstand the execution of the law, and [are] traitorously preparing, ordering and levying war against us." The king ordered all military and civil officers "to bring the traitors to justice." He went on to point out that many persons in England had carried on a "traitorous correspondence" with American rebels. He commanded every subject to aid him in bringing such traitors to trial.[85] Parliament put its stamp of approval on the doctrine announced in the proclamation. The Prohibitory Act, which stopped all American commerce, described the Colonies to be in "open rebellion," their actions as "rebellious and treasonable Commotions." The statute authorized the king to appoint commissioners who could extend pardons, presumably of treason, in areas that returned to peace and obedience.[86] The system of general coercion was as complete as a legislature could make it.

Events forced the English government to deal again with the problem of individual traitors. The capture of Colonel Ethan Allen during Montgomery's Canadian campaign brought the ministry face to face with a real flesh-and-blood American rebel. His captor, General Robert Prescott, had promised Allen that he would "grace a halter at Tyburn." [87] Carleton shipped Allen and thirty-three fellow prisoners to England, where, late in December, 1775, they landed at Falmouth. As soldiers led the Americans through throngs of curious folk to their prison at Pendennis Castle,[88] the ministry pondered the problem posed by Allen. Whatever treatment he received would set precedent. Was he a criminal or a prisoner of war? On December 23, the new American secretary, Lord George Germain, summoned the king's servants to determine Allen's fate. What passed at the meeting is unknown. The law officers attended, but wrote no opinion.[89] The ministers decided to treat Allen as a prisoner of war, and in less than three weeks he was at sea, bound eventually for New York and freedom.[90] Allen later stated that he won his freedom when someone sued out a writ of habeas corpus in the English courts.[91] Such action may well have been taken in collusion with the administration, for it would have furnished them with a way out of an embarrassing situation.

The real reason for the release of Allen was the certain knowledge that Americans would execute British prisoners if he suffered a traitor's death. Washington had impressed this fact upon Gage in August. Information that the British treated prisoners as criminals caused Washington to write to Gage to expect retaliation if he departed from the practices observed by nations at war.[92] Gage answered that the prisoners had received better treatment than they deserved;

Britain, "pre-eminent in mercy, [had] outgone common examples, and overlooked the criminal in the captive." He left no doubt as to the status of the prisoners, "whose lives by the law of the land are destined to the cord." [93] Washington answered Gage with an air of stern finality, announcing that his correspondence with the general was closed, "perhaps forever." [94] The threat of retaliation stood.

By proclamation and statute the administration had announced its opinion that Americans were traitors. When the course of events prevented immediate trial and execution, Parliament stepped into the breach with a statute which made possible the extended detention of American prisoners by suspending the writ of habeas corpus. The act provided that no judge or justice of the peace could bring an American to trial for treason without permission of the Privy Council. No court could release on bail an American committed for treason. The king was authorized to set aside places for the confinement of American prisoners.[95] The obvious purpose of the statute was to make possible the imprisonment of Americans during the pleasure of the ministry: if the war ended in British victory, the trip to Tyburn would be completed; if America made good her claim to independence, the prisoners would be released.

The statute operated as its authors intended in the case of Henry Laurens, whom the British had captured at sea as he was making his way to the Netherlands on a diplomatic mission.[96] The magistrates committed him to the Tower of London on a charge of high treason.[97] During his long imprisonment, the ministry tempted him with a pardon for his treason, which he refused to accept since he regarded himself as a civilian prisoner of war, guilty of no crime. The surrender of Cornwallis made Laurens a likely candidate as an exchange for the general. Yet the administration, refusing to admit that he was in fact a prisoner of war subject to exchange, played the farce out to the last act. On

December 31, 1781, they brought him before Mansfield to be released on bail.[98] Aware that posting bond might be interpreted as an admission of guilt, Laurens conditioned the act by saying:

I know not the nature of the obligation which is to be required of me, therefore I think it necessary to make this previous declaration, that I hold myself to be a citizen of the United, free and independent States of North America, and will not do any act which shall involve me in an acknowledgment of subjection to this realm.[99]

Ministerial attempts to apply the English law of treason to America failed dismally. Efforts to bring persons to trial in the Colonies were frustrated by American unwillingness to participate in the proceedings. The idea of bringing Americans to England for trial aroused Colonial hostility because it violated local control of the judicial process, a right for which the colonists had long contended. Fear of retaliation put an emphatic period to all attempts to try individuals. The policy of declaring Colonial areas to be in rebellion proved to be not only futile, but disastrous to the empire. The coercive measures that such declarations justified drove the Colonies from a struggle for constitutional rights to an armed struggle for independence.

3

National and State Origins
of the American Law of Treason

The origins of the American law of treason were national, developing from the experience of the Continental Army between June, 1775 and June, 1776. August, 1775 found Washington in a difficult, delicate situation. He commanded an army under the authority of the Continental Congress. Yet the Congress had shown itself unwilling to act in critical areas where inaction meant certain defeat. Such an area was the control of disaffected persons. Had it faced the problem of disloyalty squarely, Congress would have had to act vigorously against the friends of George III, the sovereign to whom a majority of members professed loyalty until as late as the summer of 1776.

Having created an army, Congress had to provide for its regulation. Here the issue of disloyalty could not be avoided. Men who joined the American army were under the ban of the English law. They had dissolved the bonds of allegiance and were "destined to the cord." By translating into action their faith in a cause, they became the first American citizens. They announced boldly a new allegiance, a breach of which constituted treason against America.

The first legislative act that authorized the punishment of Americans guilty of treasonable practices was the law establishing the articles of war of the Continental Army, passed by Congress June 30, 1775. Articles five and six authorized the punishment of mutiny and sedition, the military equivalent of levying war against the state. Articles twenty-six through twenty-eight made criminal the following: providing the enemy with supplies, harboring an enemy, and corresponding with the enemy, acts analogous to the crime of adhering to the enemy, giving aid and comfort. The articles, applying only to persons under the authority of the Continental Army, recognized as criminal the two general heads of activity that the constitutional law of the United States would regard as treason. The resolves authorized such punishment as a court-martial should order, short of the death penalty.[1]

The original articles of war proved to be an inadequate tool for the task of changing the disorganized civilian crew before Boston into a real instrument of war. The difficulty of introducing discipline [2] was but one of the problems that caused Washington to call the attention of Congress to the state of the army in September, 1775.[3] In response, Congress decided to send a committee of three to confer with the general and the governors of four New England states.[4]

Before the congressional committee arrived at camp, events in Massachusetts gave the question of treason in the army new urgency. By October, a cloud of suspicion surrounded Benjamin Church, the chief surgeon of the army. Church moved in the highest Patriot circles. He sat with the Boston committee of correspondence, held a seat in the provincial congress, and since July, 1775, had been director general of army hospitals. What is now proved,[5] that Church had acted as Gage's informer as early as May, 1775, was not then even suspected until after the affair of the cypher letter. Late in September, Church wrote a coded letter to his brother-in-law, John Fleming, within the British lines at Boston. The doctor's mistress carried it through the Patriot lines. The letter miscarried and eventually came to Washington. The woman identified Church as the author. A search of his papers, previously "edited" by a friend, revealed nothing.

The method employed by Church and the fact that the letter was in cypher was more damaging than the contents. He discussed conditions in the American camp, describing them as far better than facts warranted. The possibility exists that by previous arrangement the letter would have a different, perhaps opposite, meaning to Fleming. Later a contemporary suggested that Church might have been warning the British not to mount an attack at that moment, though the general condition of the American army makes this improbable. The letter closed, "Make use of every precaution, or I perish." [6]

At a council of war held on October 4, Church, though admitting that he had written the letter, asserted that he had intended to effect a reconciliation. Washington put the question to the council "whether it did not appear that Dr. Church had carried on a criminal Correspondence with the Enemy." The generals' unanimous decision was that the act had been criminal.[7] Turning to the articles of war, the council found punishment, excepting the death penalty, to be at their discretion. The generals decided that, considering "the Enormity of the Crime," [8] the approved sentences of cashiering, whipping, fines, and brief imprisonment, were inadequate. Regarding Church as a traitor, they wanted severe punishment. The next day Washington informed Congress of Church's perfidy and suggested an amendment of the twenty-eighth article of war.[9]

Next, the Massachusetts House of Representatives took up the case. Church appeared at their bar, offering to resign. The house voted to expel him. Several weeks later the legislators resolved to take "further Measures" against the doctor if the Continental authority released him. The preamble of the resolve, following the lead of the army council, stated the conviction of the House that Church had committed treason.[10] Here Massachusetts faced a dilemma. The criminal law of the colony was based on English law. If treason consisted of betrayal of allegiance owed the king, how could they punish action in behalf of George III? To prosecute Church for treason would be the act of an independent state. Unwilling to take such a drastic step, Massachusetts turned to the Continental Congress. The speaker, James Warren, summed up the situation in a letter to John Adams: [11]

How he is to receive adequate punishment is I suppose a question for your determination. I am sensible of the deficiencies in your code of laws, and the objections to *post facto* laws; but something must be done, and he made an example of . . . Our House are adjusting the ceremonies of proceeding in order of expulsion, *and then will end our tether* [last italics mine].

News of Church's treason burst like a bomb in the Congress.[12] On October 17 he was removed from office; on November 7 Congress ordered his confinement in a Connecticut jail.[13] In the spring of 1776, Congress permitted him to return to Massachusetts for reasons of health. Sometime later he was allowed to leave the country. His ship, bound for the West Indies, apparently went down at sea.[14]

The Church affair directly influenced the congressional committee that conferred with Washington about the better regulation of the army. The committee met at Cambridge in October, during the excitement caused by Church's treachery. The committee, recommending amendments to the articles of war, advised Congress to authorize the death penalty for the military treasons of mutiny, sedition, and correspondence with the enemy.[15] So prompted, Congress stiffened the articles of war.[16] Congress, prodded by the army, took a long step toward independence by authorizing the death penalty for American soldiers who adhered to George III.

But the larger question of disaffection among the civilian population remained unsolved. By the spring of 1776, the term "traitor" had been applied frequently to the Tories. An army chaplain, addressing the troops on the occasion of the British evacuation of Boston, commented with obvious satisfaction "that the Tories were thunder-struck when orders were issued for evacuating the town. . . . Thus are many of those deluded creatures, those vile traitors to their country, obliged at last, in their turn to abandon their once delightful habitations. . . ." [17] In March, 1776, an effigy of former governor William Tryon was paraded through the streets of New York. A placard attached to the dummy described Tryon as "a professed rebel and traitor," guilty of "numberless traitorous practices against the liberties of this country." [18] Writing in the Providence *Gazette,* "Amicus Patriae" warned Patriots to beware of Tories who professed to be friends of their country. He compared them with the vilest traitor on record, Judas Iscariot.[19]

Yet, however high sentiment ran against Tories during the winter of 1775–76, the individual states refused to take upon themselves the responsibility for providing legal sanctions by defining treason.[20] Congress also avoided the issue. Control of the disaffected passed by default to the army, and for a time Washington acted without congressional authorization.

The threat of a British landing at Newport, Rhode Island, in December, 1775, caused Washington to send General Charles Lee into the state. Lee spent ten days there, over the holidays. Apparently acting on his own initiative, he administered a strong oath to the Tories. Those who took the oath swore not to supply the king's troops nor to give intelligence to the enemy. The juror swore to inform the committee of safety if he got "the knowledge of such treason." The oath ruled out neutrality, which was "as base and criminal" as adhering to the king. The juror further swore to defend the American cause with arms.[21]

Later that winter, as it seemed probable that Howe would land at New York, Lee asked Washington to send him there to prepare the defense. He asked for authority to deal sternly with the Tories, particularly those of Long Island: "Not to crush these Serpents, before their rattles are grown, would be ruinous." He reminded the commander that, since Congress would not act, he must take the initiative.[22] Washington's instructions empowered Lee to disarm New York Tories and, if necessary, to take other measures to secure them.[23] Lee informed Congress that he was off to New York to purge "all its environs of Traitors." [24]

Lee acted with his accustomed vigor. He disarmed many Tories and sent them into Connecticut as Continental prisoners. Again he administered his Rhode Island oath. His sharp action raised the issue of civil supremacy. The New York government complained to Congress, and that body resolved that in the future the military was not to impose any kind of test oath on civilians.[25] Though Congress hesitated, Washington urged Lee on.[26] Apropos of Lee's action, Washington commented, "It is high time to begin with our internal foes when we are threatened with such Severity of Chastisement from our kind Parent without." [27]

Pressed by the army, Congress took a halting step toward independence in January, 1776. In carefully worded resolves, avoiding the issue of treason and allegiance, Congress adopted part of the army program. The Tory Act was based on the theory that those who failed to support the American cause had been misled by ministerial propaganda. Congress instructed local committees to inform the population of the true nature of the American cause. If any person failed to accept the American cause, he was to be disarmed. The resolve advised the states to take the more dangerous Tories into custody and bind them with sufficient sureties. Continental troops were placed at the disposal of state authorities.[28]

Events in New York in June, 1776 hastened the development of an American law of treason. Early in the month, the Provincial Congress discovered what appeared to be a large ring of counterfeiters, involving both soldiers and civilians. Further inquiry revealed a treacherous plot: the counterfeiters received their bogus bills from the royal governor, William Tryon. They used the money to expedite the recruiting of a pro-British force in New York. The conspirators planned a rising to coincide with Howe's arrival. Rumor expanded the plot until it included a plan to assassinate Washington. Doubtless this story had its basis in the fact that one of the principals, Thomas Hickey, was a member of the general's personal guard.[29]

Acting under the articles of war, Washington brought Hickey to trial before a general court-martial. The officers found the prisoner guilty of "Sedition and mutiny, and also of holding a treacherous correspondence with the enemy." [30] The day after his trial, Hickey died on the gallows. Washington had taken a decisive step; action based on loyalty to George III had been interpreted as a heinous crime. By executing Hickey, the first American to suffer death for treason, Washington announced publicly, in an irrevocable manner, his status as the representative of an independent state.

The Hickey plot forced state and national governments to make decisions on the question of civilian traitors. After discovery of the plot, the New York government, though willing to cooperate with Washington, had refused to take any decisive action. Several of the conspirators had been state prisoners. The New York congress had decided that, since the "courts of judicature of this colony, being as yet held, by authority derived from the crown of Great Britain," they would be unable to deal with the prisoners.[31]

With the whole matter at his door, Washington informed Congress that David Mathews, the mayor of New York, had been implicated. Congress sent a secret committee to confer with the general. This committee charged Mathews with "dangerous designs and treasonable conspiracies against the rights and liberties of the United Colonies of America." [32] At the request of the committee, Washington apprehended Mathews.

News of Mathews' implication in the Hickey plot moved Congress to consider the status of civilian traitors.[33] On June 24 Congress passed three resolves: the first announced that all persons deriving protection from American laws owed allegiance to the American governments; the second and third resolves recommended that the Colonies pass laws defining treason and counterfeiting.[34]

Though these resolves could not establish a basis for the trial of Mathews, they did put the moral force of the Union behind whatever action New York chose to take against him. The state officials first had hoped that Washington would try the mayor, but since the resolves did not authorize the military trial of civilians, he took no action. Washington suggested the removal of the conspirators from the state. In July, having approved the Declaration of Independence and defined the crime of treason against the state, New York sent Mathews and five others into Connecticut.[35]

The congressional resolve of June 24 was the ultimate basis of every treason statute and prosecution during the American Revolution. In anticipation of the federal constitution it was:

Resolved, That all persons abiding within any of the United Colonies, and deriving protection from the laws of the same, owe allegiance to the said laws, and are members of such colony;

and that all persons passing through, visiting or making a temporary stay in any of the said colonies, being entitled to the protection of the laws during the time of such passage, visitation or temporary stay, owe during the same time, allegiance thereto:

That all persons, members of, or owing allegiance to any of the United Colonies, as before described, who shall levy war against any of the said colonies within the same, or be adherent to the King of Great Britain, or others the enemies of the said colonies, or any of them, within the same, giving to him or them aid and comfort, are guilty of treason against such colony:

That it be recommended to the legislatures of the several United Colonies to pass laws for punishing such persons before described, as shall be proveably [*sic*] attainted of open deed, by people of their own condition, of any of the treasons before described.

This first public act to declare George III the enemy explicitly defied the sovereign and was a *de facto* declaration of independence.[36]

Though the resolutions referred to the United Colonies, it was probably no mere coincidence that the term "United States" was used by a member of Congress the day after the treason resolve was passed. A letter of Elbridge Gerry to Horatio Gates illustrates the connection between the resolutions and independence: [37]

I think we are in a fair way to a speedy Declaration of Independency . . . Congress having yesterday . . . recommended to the Assemblies to make provision for punishing all inhabitants and other person receiving protection in any of the Colonies, who shall be found affording aid or comfort to the King of Great Britain, or other enemies of the United States of America.

The origins of the American law of treason were national. Pushed by the army, Congress moved forward from one decision to another. The Church case led to adoption of the death penalty for military traitors, and the army assumed responsibility for the first execution of a traitor,

Thomas Hickey. The implication of civilians in the Hickey plot led Congress to adopt the resolves of June 24. First Washington, then Congress, exercised a fundamental power of sovereign states by controlling treasonable action. Having formulated a policy, the national government, lacking civil courts, turned to the states and requested them to provide for the punishment of traitors.

The shaping of a treason law harmonious with republican government began with the Revolution. The problems were: to construct a law that could protect the state from disloyal acts involving a betrayal of allegiance; to limit that law so precisely that it could not be used to destroy normal political opposition; to protect the rights of accused individuals in times of high political excitement. The congressional resolves of June, 1775, showed a definite restrictive intent. When state legislators, often amateurs acting in an atmosphere of crisis, began implementing the national resolves, they wrote an erratic record.

The states, relieved of the original responsibility of assuming sovereign power, acted promptly on the congressional recommendation. Within six months of independence, six states had statutes on their books defining the crime of treason. The laws were regarded as fundamental, as a main support of the newly declared independence.[38] Having declared levying war against the state and adherence to be treason, the question necessarily followed, what did the ancient words mean in the new jurisdictions? The preamble of one statute pointed up this imperfect understanding with its opening clause, "divers opinions may be what cases shall be adjudged treason, and what not." [39]

Three methods of defining the law were employed by the legislatures. The first was to incorporate into the law of the state the common law under this head. The second was to describe in the treason statutes what acts would constitute levying war and adherence. The third alternative was to pass statutes establishing as crimes less than treason, action that under common law would have been treason.

Undoubtedly the common law would be one source of definitive information. Maryland left the door to the use of English precedent wide open by providing that the crimes declared treasonable were to "receive the same construction that have been given to such of the said crimes as are enumerated in the statute of Edward the third, commonly called the statute of treason." New Jersey, New York, and Delaware authorized the use of English common and statute law in their constitutions.[40] Basically, though, the degree to which English precedent would influence American law was to depend on the opinions of state judges.[41]

The legislative effort to define the old English terms was most comprehensive in relation to acts that would constitute adhering to the enemy, giving him aid and comfort. By ordinance or statute, New York, Pennsylvania, Massachusetts, Maryland, New Hampshire, and Virginia repeated or paraphrased the words of the statute of Edward III.[42] At least four states attempted more specific definitions of adherence as well as aid and comfort. In 1777, Pennsylvania revised her earlier ordinances and defined adherence to include: joining the army of the enemy or persuading others to join, furnishing the enemy with arms or other supplies, or carrying on a "traitorous correspondence" with the enemy. North Carolina, Connecticut, and New Jersey defined adherence similarly. In effect, these statutes described adherence so broadly as to include virtually all forms of cooperation with the British. They went beyond Colonial and English concepts of adherence, for example, by making trading with the enemy treason.

All of the states regarded levying war as treasonable. At face value the words conveyed a clear meaning—to attempt by violence to overthrow the government. At English law the character of levying war had been much extended by the judges and included aggravated riots that tried to stop the execution of a general law. Presumably, the doctrine of constructed war prevailed in those states (Maryland, New Jersey, New York, Delaware), that had formally received the common law. A Pennsylvania law passed late in the Revolution probably belongs in the category of a constructive levying of war. The statute made it high treason to attempt to erect an independent government within the boundaries of the commonwealth.[43]

The provision of the statute of Edward III that had made compassing or imagining the death of the king treason had been used subsequently by English judges to cover written or spoken subversive words and conspiracies to levy war. Since the American states had no personal symbol of sovereignty, the compassing clause was not included in the statutes. In most instances it is not clear whether the legislators realized that they were also excluding a substantial area of common law treason.

In drafting a general criminal statute for Virginia in 1778, Thomas Jefferson made it clear in his notes that he understood the relation of the statute of Edward III to the judicially constructed treasons that developed later. His draft statute included levying war and adherence as treason "and no others" in order to "prevent an inundation of common law treasons." [44]

Five states included conspiracies to levy war or plots to betray the state in the list of treasonable acts.[45] In English law, the point at which words, spoken or written, would be regarded as treasonable had always been a vexed question. Several of the states, as noted, included attempts to persuade persons to enlist in the British armies as acts of adherence. Some states also classified corresponding with the enemy as treason. Only one state, New Hampshire, made the maintenance of opinion, as such, treason. A statute of 1781 made any-

one who wrote that the king had authority in the state subject to the penalties for the high crime.[46]

In addition to the laws defining treason, the states studded
their statute books with laws punishing a wide variety of
Tory activities. In a sense, these laws helped to limit the law
of treason by establishing many disloyal acts as less than treasonable.[47] The Virginia statute described such acts as "inferior in malignity to treason" but "injurious to the Independence of America." [48] The anti-Tory acts covered a wide
range: acknowledging the sovereignty of the king; persuading persons to abandon their allegiance; discouraging persons from enlisting in the American forces; advising persons
to submit in the event of invasion; drinking the king's health;
speaking or writing against government; spreading discouraging rumors; inciting disorders; giving intelligence to the
enemy. In two states, New York and South Carolina, such
ancillary crimes were described as felonies.[49] Since a felony
carried the death penalty, these were cases where names did
not change the nature of things. It made very little difference
whether one hanged as a traitor or a felon. In most instances,
though, these statutes prescribed lesser punishments such as
fines, imprisonment, deportation, and involuntary military
service.[50] These laws were an early example of what was to
be a recurring pattern of American legislation—stringent
wartime measures which regard as less than treasonable acts
that interfere with the war effort. Such laws may seriously
abridge principles of civil liberty as those principles are understood in time of peace. At least they produce no "bloody
assize."

Definitions of the substantive criminal law are of little
value to a person accused of crime unless the law establishes
clearly his specific procedural rights. While the English substantive law tended toward severity, the procedural law in-
creased the security of the individual. Though there had been
some earlier procedural guarantees, the definitive English

statute regulating trials of treason was passed in 1696.[51] This tendency toward greater procedural security was extended by the American legislatures.

Several state courts were given jurisdiction in treason cases. The general rule prescribed that such cases should be tried by the Supreme Court *en banc* or at the circuit. Such assignment of cases corresponded to the English rule, for the county courts there did not have jurisdiction in treason cases. The pressures of war made necessary some exceptions to the rule of trying treason in the higher courts.[52]

Two commissions carried by judges on circuit gave them authority to try treason cases. The commission of general gaol delivery empowered the courts to bring to trial all persons indicted, but not tried. The commission of oyer and terminer authorized the court to summon grand juries and try the indictments found. The special commission of oyer and terminer was particularly well adapted to the needs of state governments during the war. At least four states authorized its use.[53] Advantages of this commission were that it could be used at any time at the discretion of the executive, thus bringing quick justice to traitors; it allowed a choice of justices; [54] it could be used to relieve pressure in the terribly overcrowded jails between regular visits of the assize justices.

Substantial changes were made in the matter of pleading, or failing to plead, on indictment. Though the provisions varied widely from state to state, the general tendency was toward greater security relative to forced pleas.[55] Automatic condemnation as a traitor awaited the person who stood mute at indictment in two states.[56] Two others modified the English law to the advantage of the accused.[57] If a person accused of treason refused to plead, a jury decided whether he stood mute from malice or act of God. If the jurors found he stood mute by act of God, the prisoner was confined until he recovered. If the refusal was fraudulent, a plea of "not guilty" was entered. New York made a definite move toward a more humanitarian law by forbidding the barbarous practice of the *peine fort et dure,* a process by which weights were added to the body of a mute until he pleaded or died. Standing mute in New York amounted to a proper plea of not guilty.

The states adopted most of the provisions of the Trial of Treasons Act. For example, the right to counsel, not extended to all felons in England until 1837, was guaranteed by three states.[58] Two adopted practically all of the statute of 1696, including the right to a list of the panel, compulsory process for the accused, a limitation on the right of the government to challenge jurors peremptorily.[59]

That part of the English act referring to evidence was the summation of years of wrangling about the nature of proper evidence in treason trials.[60] The statute contained provisions about both heads of evidence, that is, the number of witnesses required to prove the crime, and the type of information that could be given in evidence:

. . . no person whatsoever shall be indicted, tried or attainted of High Treason . . . but by and upon the Oaths and Testimony of Two lawful Witnesses, either both of them to the same overt act or one of them to one and one to another act of the same Treason, unless the party indicted and arraigned or tried shall willingly without force or violence in open Court confess the same. . . .

The effect of these requirements was "to secure the subject from being sacrificed to fictitious conspiracies, which have been the engines of profligate and crafty politicians in all ages." [61]

The Continental Congress recommended that the states require the testimony of more than one person to an overt act. Traitors were to be "proveably [*sic*] attainted of open deed, by people of their own condition." State legislatures accepted this recommendation. Pennsylvania required two witnesses, not necessarily to the same overt act. New Jersey copied the words of the congressional resolution almost verbatim. Virginia required two witnesses to an open deed, Maryland two witnesses to each fact charged in the indictment. New York adopted the rules of evidence of English law. Massachusetts repeated the provisions of the English statute of 1696. These rules regulating evidence were a guarantee of personal liberty and as such were to become a part of the constitutional law of the United States.[62]

The states made many innovations in the consequences of judgment in treason proceedings. At common law the immediate consequence of judgment was attainder, which, in effect, anticipated punishment. One attainted of treason was civilly dead. The inevitable consequences of attainder were twofold. First, the personal and real property of the attainted was forfeited to the crown. This included all lands, rights of entry, and profits from land. The second consequence was corruption of the blood. This meant that the attainted person could not inherit land or other hereditaments, nor bequeath them, nor could his posterity obtain property if its title descended through him.[63]

All states forfeited the estate of the attainted traitor. There was, however, a marked tendency to limit the effects of judgment to the condemned and to prevent the incidental punishment of his relatives. Pennsylvania and North Carolina authorized their judges to make provision for dependents out of the forfeited estate. Virginia saved the widow's dower in land. In three states, specific statutory provisions barred any corruption of the blood.[64]

The humanitarian tendencies of the American law are well illustrated by changes made in the method of putting traitors to death. The punishment prescribed by English law was hideous: [65]

1. That the offender be drawn to the gallows, and not be carried or walk; though usually (by connivance at length ripened by

humanity into law) a sledge or hurdle is allowed . . . 2. That he be hanged by the neck and then cut down alive. 3. That his entrails be taken out and burned, while he is yet alive. 4. That his head be cut off. 5. That his body be divided into four parts. 6. That his head and quarters be at the King's disposal.

Without exception the American states reduced the punishment of a condemned traitor to simple hanging. The New York law announced that the change was made because:

the judgment directed by the law of England, now in force in this State, in all cases of High Treason . . . are, so far as they Respect the Manner of putting the Offender to Death; marked by Circumstances of Savage Cruelty, unnecessary for the Purpose of public Justice, and manifestly repugnant to that Spirit of Humanity, which should ever distinguish a free, a civilized, and Christian People.[66]

4

The Times That
Tried Men's Souls

Executive and judicial departments of the new state governments were slow to act under the statutes establishing and
defining the crime of treason. In many states there are no
treason trials on record. Though officials kept busy prosecuting Tories under the many statutes limiting their activity,
only on the greatest provocation would enforcement ma-
chinery be set in motion to accuse persons of, and try them
for, treason. From the standpoint of the commission of the
great crime, the question of loyalty became real only when
the armies were in action. Treason was an incident of battle.

The New England treason statutes were all but dead
letters. Most military action there antedated the Declaration
of Independence and the statutes establishing the crime.
Many potential traitors accompanied Howe to Halifax. This,
together with the loyalty to the Patriot cause of the overwhelming majority of New Englanders, explains the small
number of treason trials in the area.

The only person known to have suffered death for high
treason in New England was Moses Dunbar of Connecticut.
Dunbar moved to Long Island early in the war and sometime later accepted a commission in the Tory regiment of
Colonel Edmund Fanning. A visit to his home state proved
to be his undoing. After investigation, two justices of the

peace committed him to Hartford jail, charged with high treason. A superior court jury was satisfied that Dunbar had enlisted in the king's army, had regularly received pay from Howe, and had enlisted at least one other man in the British service. Convicted and condemned, Dunbar temporarily cheated the hangman, when one Elisha Wadsworth engineered his escape. He was soon recaptured, and the state took his life among a "prodigious concourse of People." [1]

At the same session the state won a conviction against Wadsworth on a charge of "treasonable practices." [2] Another, Gurdon Whitman, escaped the gallows when the court set aside a verdict of guilty on his motion for an arrest of judgment.[3] Connecticut authorities later committed seventeen of Dunbar's associates on charges of treason, but apparently never brought them to trial.[4]

During the summer of 1776, news of the southward advance of a British army stationed in Canada alarmed the residents of New Hampshire. Many thought that the British advance would be irresistible. Prudence seemed to dictate some declaration of loyalty to the king. So motivated, several men, including one Asa Porter, crossed into New York and contacted the British forces. The committees of safety of Haverhill and Newbury interrupted the business at this point. Sitting as a court of inquiry, they sent Porter on to higher authorities where the decision was made to hold him for trial before the state legislature. Regarding himself as charged with treason, Porter argued in a long petition that the legislature had no jurisdiction. Knowing that his neighbors had shared his fears, he offered to return to Haverhill and stand trial before a jury of the vicinage according to the law of England. The legislature escaped this dilemma by confining Porter to the farm of a Massachusetts relative, taking surety for his good behavior.[5]

The occasional charges of treason levied in Massachusetts seem never to have been brought to the conclusion of a conviction. In May, 1777, Boston officials committed one Smith, alias Williamson, on a charge of treason.[6] The association of the noted Tory Dr. Samuel Stearns with Thomas Gleason, a counterfeiter and all-round rogue, brought a charge of treason at Worcester. Bound by a recognizance of £100,000 the doctor forfeited it and moved to New York.[7] The perennial agitations of Samuel Ely caused a charge of "treasonable practices" to be levied against him. The result is obscure, but the record indicates that he continued his agitation.[8]

The first large-scale trials came in New Jersey, a consequence of Washington's retreat and counterattack. As Howe moved ponderously across the state, men came in to accept the pardon offered in his proclamation of November 30. Many enlisted in the British service, and loyalist regiments were formed. Farmers supplied the royal troops with provisions and information. Substantial portions of New Jersey remained disaffected throughout the war. Even when the state was not the scene of major military operations, its residents were exposed to attack. Bergen and parts of Essex County remained Tory havens so long as the British held New York City. The long coastline invited cooperation. The situation improved somewhat after Clinton passed through New Jersey on his way from Philadelphia to New York during the summer of 1778.[9]

After Washington's twin victories at Trenton and Princeton, the civil government of New Jersey resumed operations. The legislature had fallen back before the British attack and dissolved under pressure in the southern corner of the state. Now the council of safety, assuming the functions of government, directed a concerted attack against traitors.[10] It is no longer possible to reconstruct in any detail the treasonable acts of persons brought to justice in New Jersey.[11] Evidently only flagrant acts of disaffection, direct aid to the enemy army, ended in charges of treason. The council of safety moved about the state, holding preliminary hearings. The councilors determined whether the evidence would support the charge of treason, and committed suspected persons to jail.[12] Later the justices cleared the jails by holding courts of oyer and terminer. Though the conclusion of many cases is now obscure, there are scattering evidences of the death penalty.[13]

The most influential man in the drive against traitors was the popular Patriot governor, William Livingston. Though no terrorist, he stood for a policy of stern justice, regarding a traitor in New Jersey as *"Satan among the sons of God."* [14] The Tories had been forewarned by his proclamation of February, 1777, which enjoined the justices of the peace strictly to enforce the act to punish traitors.[15] During the same month he sent a strong speech to the General Assembly.[16] This eloquent indictment was a solemn warning to the Tories. Moved by avarice or fear, disloyalists hoped to be rewarded. But, said Livingston, their hopes would turn to ashes; they would be "told by their haughty masters that they indeed approved of the Treason, but despised the Traitor." Moving to his peroration, he urged the legislators to:

use all their Influence and Authority to rouse the supine; to animate the irresolute, to confirm the wavering; and to draw from his lurking Hole, the sculking [*sic*] Neutral, who, leaving to others the Heat and Burden of the Day, means in the final Result to reap the Fruits of that Victory for which he will not contend. Let us be peculiarly assiduous, in bringing to condign Punishment, these detestable Parricides, who have been openly active against their native Country. And may we . . . in due Time, avenge an injured People, on their unfeeling oppressor, and his bloody Instruments.

As late as the spring of 1779, Livingston advised the Assembly not to adopt the policy of leniency advocated by the Continental Congress.[17] He reminded the legislators that the thirty-one traitors whom the state had pardoned on condition of enlisting in the army had deserted "to a man." He thought lives would have been saved and misery prevented had the state "treated [its] bosom-traitors with proper severity." [18]

In January of 1779 the chief justice, coming home from the circuit, wrote to Livingston and expressed the hope that no further examples would be needed in cases of treason. He thought New Jersey government to be so stabilized "that nothing remained but to forgive." [19] As the British eased the pressure of war in the north and shifted their main effort to the south, judicial proceedings slackened. The day of large-scale treason trials in New Jersey was over; the hope of Justice Symmes a reality.

Throughout the war the strategic importance of New York made the state a real or potential battleground. Disloyalty came early with the armies, and military activity became treason's barometer. In 1776, as Washington retreated north from Manhattan Island, the civil government moved along ahead of the armies. The committee to detect conspiracies cleared the jails along the Hudson, sending suspected traitors into New England. The state brought few, or none, of these men to trial.[20]

A year later the threat of British attack caused New York to quicken its proceedings against traitors even though the state still had no regular government. The convention, while it drafted a constitution, acted as a provisional government. To the ordinary problems of government were added the urgent ones of supply and defense.

The military situation looked desperate. New Yorkers feared a concerted attack from north and south along the Hudson-Champlain line. The northern frontier was held precariously. All expected Carleton to try again the descent to Albany. Brant and Butler stirred up the western Indians. In the face of this, Schuyler and Gates fought their feud for the command of the northern department. The New York government feared a Tory rising in support of a two-pronged British invasion. This was no fantasy born of hysteria; prominent loyalists were with Howe in the city, planning Tory action. British-sponsored agents infiltrated Ulster, Westchester, Orange, Albany, and Tryon counties, offering protection and enlisting men. Groups of Tories broke through Patriot lines to go over to Howe. Persons of dubious loyalty filled the inadequate jails. County committees clamored for a general jail delivery. In these perilous times, the legislature turned to the military to clear its jails of the disaffected and to break a formidable Tory plot. By resolutions passed in March and April, the convention empowered courts-martial to try spies and traitors.[21]

First action came from General Alexander McDougall who commanded at Peekskill, the extreme southern position on the left bank of the Hudson. To the south lay the "neutral ground," an area in which neither American nor British arms held a sufficient advantage to maintain order. Here men lived in an atmosphere of corrosive distrust. Loyalty shifted with the ebb and flow of rumors from the city. British agents enlisted men; small groups filtered through the lines to join Howe. The first to be tried was Simon Mabee,[22] who had been found by an American scouting party in the house of a suspected Tory. A close search revealed an enlistment warrant and a certification that Mabee had taken an oath of allegiance to George III. The prisoner disclaimed any knowledge of the papers and offered the opinion that they had arrested the wrong Simon Mabee. Another one, of Dutchess County, had been missing for some time, he said. The officers, finding him guilty of being employed by the enemy and enlisting men in the British service, sentenced him to hang.

Next, McDougall's court tried John Williams. Several witnesses testified that Williams was a British recruiting

Agent. He had offered each prospect twenty dollars, a suit of clothes, and a land bounty of one hundred acres; he had urged the recruits to make haste as the British invasion was imminent. To the allegation of one witness, that he had seen Williams enter a man's name on a muster roll, the accused answered that he could not write. He described the testimony against him as "all Romance." Six character witnesses could not tip the scale in his favor, and the court sentenced him to hang.[23] The court then condemned Job Babcock, one of Williams' recruits.[24] Anthony Hill, who had been taken north of King's Bridge, was charged with enlisting men in the British service. Hill claimed that he had accepted the enlistment warrant in order to get out of New York City. He had tried to destroy the warrant, but his captors had pieced it together. The court refused to accept his declaration of good intention and sentenced him to death.[25]

The last court-martial held under McDougall's authority met in June, 1777. John Likely and Anthony Umans stood charged with adhering to the king of Great Britain. They had been caught in a carefully baited trap: several ardent Whigs went to their homes, posed as Tories on their way through the lines to New York, and both Likely and Umans gave the men instructions as to the safest route through the American positions. Found guilty, they were sentenced by the court to receive one hundred lashes and to be imprisoned for the duration of the war.[26]

Across the Hudson, General George Clinton held a court-martial at Fort Montgomery late in April. News of concerted pro-British activity had reached the convention earlier in the month. The commissioners for detecting conspiracies were ordered to turn over to Clinton the more dangerous persons in their custody. The main group of criminals tried by Clinton were the associates of Jacobus Rosa.

Rosa, a resident of Marbletown, enlisted men in Ulster

and Orange counties for service in Fanning's royalist regiment, offering cash and land bounties as bait. He warned those he contacted that Howe would be up the river as soon as the grass was long enough to forage the cavalry. Toward the end of April he gathered his company, about thirty-six strong, and tried to pass the American lines. They met their first opposition at the Wall Kill in Ulster County. In overwhelming a tiny militia guard that tried to block their way, Rosa's party aroused the countryside. The desperate group hurried on to the south, past Bethlehem, over the Orange County line into a hilly area known as the "Clove." Here a short fight with the militia broke them up, and the Americans took several prisoners.

An eighteen man court-martial sat at Fort Montgomery to try the prisoners. Ten men were charged with levying war against the state, adhering to the king, and being enlisted in his service while owing allegiance to New York. In addition, the ringleaders, Rosa and Jacob Middagh, were charged with enlisting men in the British service. Both men pleaded guilty to all the charges except that of enlisting men. Evidently the actual enlistment was not to take place until the party reached New York. Rosa, confident that British arms would effect his release before the New York law had run its course, talked freely of his exploits. A second group of Rosa's adherents stood trial early in May. In all, the court sentenced thirty to hang and acquitted eight. Eventually all of the guilty except two received pardons. Only Rosa and Middagh were hanged.[27]

A similar pattern, aggravated by the danger of Indian attack, developed in the northern counties. As in the south, pro-British agents circulated with enlistment papers. Many left home and drifted off to the north to meet the British forces; others remained at home, refusing to obey the militia call. Early in April, the Albany committee wrote to the state convention imploring them to take action against the disaffected. They reminded the convention that the state had an unused resolution defining treason on its books: [28]

There has not been a time since the commencement of these troubles, that required a law to carry this resolution into execution more than the present. Our jails are full—if banished, they are returned—punishment we cannot inflict—among us they ought not to be.

Through late April the Albany militia, directed by county and special committees, rounded up British sympathizers. In the convention, John Jay prepared an "act of grace" which offered pardon to all persons guilty of treason who came in and took the oath of allegiance to New York.[29] Orders then went out to General Peter Ten Broeck to hold a court-martial.

The court sat through May and June, trying thirty-one men charged with treason. Most of the prisoners had been involved in the schemes of James Heutson and his lieutenant, Arnout Viele. Heutson tendered persons oaths of allegiance to George III. His recruits held themselves ready to aid the British when they arrived in the vicinity of Albany. Other groups had been captured as they proceeded north to meet the British. Many of the accused swore that they had no intention of taking up arms against America. Burgoyne's advance seemed irresistible, and they sought protection. It was a desperate game of self-interest in which men gambled their lives on the outcome. The court meted out punishment varying from fines of fifteen dollars to death by hanging. Some were pardoned or permitted to take advantage of the act of grace. Only Heutson and Viele were hanged.[30]

Sir William Howe's occupation of Philadelphia set the stage for a series of treason trials in Pennsylvania. Action against the disaffected started when news of Howe's landing at Head of Elk reached Philadelphia. Cooperating with the

Continental Congress, the Pennsylvania council sent off thirty-one suspected Quakers to Virginia. Several prominent men who had held office under the crown were also removed. From October, 1777 to June, 1778, Lancaster was the seat of Pennsylvania government. The supreme executive council reorganized itself into a council of safety, a body with sweeping powers of trial and punishment in cases of disloyalty.[31] Sporadically this provisional government moved against persons suspected of treasonable action.[32] During the period of exile, Pennsylvania suffered war on two fronts. The problem of treason in the western counties presented itself forcibly to the council during the spring of 1778. Tories there cooperated with Indian tribes directed by British agents from Niagara and Detroit. In Bedford County, a group of Tories led by Alexander McKee, an old hand at frontier intrigue, went off to join a mixed force of English and Indians. After this group had been captured by the militia, the council issued a special commission of oyer and terminer to try persons involved.[33]

In the east, the British occupation of Philadelphia presented the Tories with treasonable opportunities. Months before the clatter of Morgan's cavalry in the streets of the capital announced to anxious inhabitants the return of the Patriot government, the exiled council and assembly had planned legal action against disloyalists. The assembly led off by passing a sweeping confiscation act. The law also specifically attainted thirteen men, including: Joseph Galloway; Andrew, John, and William Allen; and Jacob Duche.[34]

The Continental Congress intervened to assist Pennsylvania's shattered government with the Tory problem around Philadelphia. A congressional resolution made civilians liable to court-martial if they indulged in "traitorous practices."[35] Brigadier General John Lacey of the Bucks militia seized many persons going into Philadelphia who came within the scope of the resolve. Washington agreed to try the more notorious offenders if necessary. More agreeable to the commander in chief, however, was the prospect of ultimate civil trial. Eventually Lacey tried a group of the prisoners himself. On the advice of Washington, he turned the more dangerous over to the Pennsylvania council with a recommendation to confine them during the campaign of 1778.[36]

An urgent demand for retaliation was expressed immediately after the American reoccupation of Philadelphia. Action against those who had betrayed their allegiance took every form from mob violence to solemn trials before the highest courts of the commonwealth. As soon as they returned to the capital, the supreme executive council proclaimed as traitors persons who failed to come in within a specified time to stand trial for their treasons. The list continued to lengthen and eventually 450 persons were condemned in this way.[37] Early in July, Peter Deshong, against whom process of attainder by proclamation had been started, returned to stand trial. A mob armed with clubs sought him out, but Deshong slipped away. A jury later acquitted him.[38]

The army and navy brought their traitors to account. The Pennsylvania navy tried Samuel Lyons, Samuel Ford, John Wilson, and John Lawrence on the charge of deserting to the enemy. The council, after reviewing the sentences, pardoned Wilson and Lawrence. Lyons and Ford were executed aboard a vessel near Market Street wharf.[39] In August, Benedict Arnold ordered a court-martial to try George Spangler and Frederick Verner. Spangler was hanged. In the case of Verner, the Continental Congress referred the matter to the Pennsylvania council which in turn sought the opinion of Chief Justice McKean. McKean advised setting aside the military verdict. The council held Verner for civil trial.[40]

But these proceedings were mere preliminaries to the

long-anticipated September sessions of the court of oyer and terminer and general gaol delivery for the city and county of Philadelphia. As the court sat, the city rocked with a political controversy intimately connected to the whole question of disaffection. The government in power defended the Constitution of 1776 and regarded themselves as the true Patriot party. The taint of Toryism was attached to the opposition who numbered among their adherents conservative Quakers and others who had favored the British connection.[41]

The grand jury at the September assize considered forty-five bills of indictment. Twenty-three cases came before the court which was presided over by McKean, assisted by William A. Atlee and John Evans.[42] Attorney General Jonathan D. Sergeant and Joseph Reed conducted the prosecution. The accused had able counsel in James Wilson, George Ross, and William Lewis. The extended argument of counsel and the opinions of the chief justice showed a learned bench and bar thoroughly familiar with English precedent.[43] The jury acquitted all but two of the prisoners.

The trials of Abraham Carlisle and John Roberts are the *causes célèbres* of the Revolution. Both Quakers, they had entered the service of Howe during the occupation of Philadelphia. Carlisle had acted as a gatekeeper and issued passes to those coming into the city. Roberts had given the army direct aid by recruiting men and furnishing supplies. The court sentenced both men to hang.[44]

Great pressure was brought to bear on the council to pardon the men. Petitions poured in from all sides.[45] The council remained adamant, and the state took the lives of the two men on November 4. The question of the wisdom and justice of these executions has been a moot one.[46] None would deny that Roberts and Carlisle were the proper objects of pity, but the case for mercy is less convincing. They had a fair trial before a court of moderate men who showed themselves willing to hear every argument of the learned counsel engaged to defend them. A jury of their peers found them guilty of acts clearly treasonable by known and established law. The justice of the sentences cannot be doubted.

No callous disregard of human life caused the council to reject the mercy pleas. Circumstances pointed to the need for execution. The punishments were exemplary. The pardon of Carlisle and Roberts would have amounted to a virtual guarantee of amnesty to all who contemplated treason. A group of the more ardent Patriots had been willing to avenge treason by acts of lawlessness against Peter Deshong. The great riot at the home of James Wilson, chief counsel for the traitors, showed that fears of repeated acts of violence would not have been imaginary.

The autumn assize at Philadelphia marked the high point in the concentration of the trials of traitors in Pennsylvania. After these dramatic trials, moderate leaders were able to use the policy of proscription to satisfy the demand for retaliation. The state officials did not, however, permit the treason law to become meaningless. Until the end of the Revolution the state prosecuted a few suspected traitors in all parts of the commonwealth.[47]

The trial of traitors in Pennsylvania had come in the wake of the British army. Clinton's evacuation of Philadelphia signaled the beginning of a series of brief but dramatic legal proceedings. In that summer of 1778 the situation was ripe for a bloody repression. The Patriot party had suffered stinging defeat and endured rigorous exile. Tory Philadelphians had lived in comfort, some in luxury, during the winter of Valley Forge. The desire for revenge had been so strong that extreme Whigs, impatient with the slowness of regular justice, had tried to take the law into their own hands. Yet there was no reign of terror, no drumhead justice dispensed. The state tried the men at a solemn assize where learned lawyers searched the ancient books to find the precedents of common and statute law to protect the accused. Seen in the context of the troubled times, the policy of the government of Pennsylvania toward its traitors seems moderate. The trials were examples of justice, not political reprisals.

Maryland, split in half by Chesapeake Bay, and pierced by deep and navigable rivers, lay open to British sea power. Her citizens enjoyed little security; the loyalty of whole counties wavered in the wake of British naval and military action. The Tories of the eastern shore gave authorities trouble intermittently throughout the war. By the opening months of 1777, the counties of Somerset and Worcester verged on anarchy. Tory action there, piracy and robbery mixed with loyalism, assumed the proportions of an insurrection in February with British vessels openly aiding the rebels. The rising was suppressed by a mixed force of Continentals and militia,[48] and a legislative amnesty was extended to all but a few ringleaders. Of those excepted from pardon, Smallwood captured all but Hamilton Callilo and Thomas Moore. Callilo was later pursued to an outlawry. Of those captured, some were let to bail while others remained in jail to await trial.[49]

In May the council issued a special commission of oyer and terminer which created a court in Queen Anne's County to try the insurgents.[50] Somerset and Worcester remained unpacified and further arrests were made. A second commission of oyer and terminer ordered trials to be held in Talbot County.[51] Since the commissioners for Queen Anne's had not acted, all the prisoners were concentrated for trial under the Talbot commission. In February, 1778, the council appointed Luther Martin attorney general and ordered him to prosecute before the Talbot court. The issue of the trials, if they were ever held, is unknown.[52] The Eastern Shore continued to be troubled. Howe's landing at Head of Elk in 1777 brought the inevitable cooperation with and enlistment in British forces. The state brought a group of these traitors to justice through outlawry proceedings.[53] A minor rising in Queen Anne's produced a treason conviction and an acquittal at the September, 1778 session of the general court.[54]

The most ambitious Tory plot in Maryland came in the last year of the war, an incident of Cornwallis' campaign. The Associated Loyalists of America planned joint action between the general and Maryland Tories. The agent of the association, John Caspar Frietschie, moved about the state enlisting men. His business proceeded well enough until an associate revealed the plot to a militia captain. The captain played his hand with skill, informing the council of the plot while leading the Tories to believe that he was one of them. The council issued warrants, the militia made the arrests, and the plot collapsed. A special commission of oyer and terminer sat at Fredericktown in July. The jury returned "guilty" verdicts in seven cases. Three men, including Frietschie, were hanged; four were pardoned.[55]

Maryland, exposed to the depredations of British sea power and fearful of invasion, pursued a moderate policy. The only men known to have been executed as traitors were citizens of the state who had accepted and acted upon British commissions.

Virginia loyalists were suppressed early in the war, and the Tory party, if it deserves the name, remained leaderless, scattered, and impotent. Yet the name "Tory" appears regularly in the state records. This apparent inconsistency arose from the fact that men called all who were disaffected "Tories," though opposition to government was not synonymous with loyalty to Great Britain. The great draft riots of 1781 are examples of disaffection that had little connection with the cause of George III.

Four years of war, with its steady drain on men, money, and supplies, created widespread unrest in Virginia. The militia draft of 1780–81 became the straw on the backs of a burdened people that they refused to bear. The attempt to execute the draft set off a series of riots throughout the state. In several counties, courts-martial tried the rioters for some offense less than treason.[56] In Augusta County, local officials charged the leading rioters with treason. The only regular Virginia court having jurisdiction in treason cases was the general court at Richmond. Local authorities suggested a special commission of oyer and terminer, but the council declined to act.[57] In Hampshire County the leading rioter, John Claypole, harangued the malcontents; he damned the Congress and drank a bumper to the king. This defiance brought out the sheriff, but Claypole successfully resisted arrest, and the rioters remained at large until a force of militia could be embodied. Forty-two prisoners were taken by the militia. The county court sent three to Richmond for trial and bound the rest over to appear before the grand jury. Four men were commissioned by the council to sit as a special court of oyer and terminer in Hampshire. On August 10, 1781, the date set for the trial, residents witnessed "aged mothers, wives, and children crowding to the Court house to take the last Leave of their unhappy sons, husbands, and fathers." All believed that "Execution would be immediate on the Sentence of Death." [58] The budding tragedy ended on a farcical note. The court never sat because the commissioners never arrived. A single pardon reached all the rioters except Claypole and the leaders. Eventually they, too, were pardoned.[59]

Benedict Arnold introduced Virginians to real war toward the end of 1780 with a dashing raid up the James River that ended in the sack of Richmond. Through the spring he raided continuously from his base at Portsmouth. By May, as the Revolution moved to its climax, Cornwallis was on Virginia soil. Once again British military operations convinced many that expediency dictated betrayal of allegiance owed Virginia. This attitude was succinctly expressed by a farmer accused of treason, "he would not take up arms in defence of his country, but would stay by his property and make the best terms he could." [60] As Cornwallis moved toward Yorktown, British privateers stepped up their activities along Virginia's defenseless coasts. Several prosecutions resulted when Virginians cooperated with these raiders.[61]

So long as the British had an effective force on Virginia soil, the state could do little to bring its traitors to justice. Occasionally, the council brought a notorious disloyalist to book with a court-martial.[62] Yorktown let loose a torrent of treason prosecutions that clogged the calendars of Virginia courts for months. The method of procedure dictated by state law greatly hampered the prosecutors. In accordance with the regular law, all trials of treason had to be held before the general court, sitting at Richmond. The great difficulty of transporting witnesses made the hearing of many cases by this method impracticable. Emergency legislation had empowered the council to issue special commissions of oyer and terminer. Violence at the county level and the disinclination of persons to accept the commission again made this method of trial ineffective.[63]

In November, county officials sent lists of suspected traitors to the council. Only the most notorious offenders, those who had joined the enemy or borne arms against Virginia, were detained.[64] Through the year 1782, the council ordered the worst offenders to Richmond for trial. The state won many convictions, though the exact number can no longer be determined.[65] The legislature, spreading wide the mantle of oblivion, pardoned all those sentenced to hang by the general court.[66] Not a single traitor was hanged in Virginia during the Revolution.[67]

5

The Law in Action

The historians of loyalism, implying persecution, have left a false impression concerning procedural rights during the Revolution.[1] They generalized too much on statutory evidence. Faced with overwhelming problems of governmental organization, many legislatures modified procedure, particularly in relation to jurisdiction. Reading the statutes only, one might conclude that most traitors were accused by special committees acting under the motivation of the witch-hunter and were given either drumhead justice by courts-martial or prejudged trials by special commissions of oyer and terminer. The record leads to contrary conclusions.

Though the legislatures tampered with jurisdiction, the great majority of cases were tried before supreme courts or at the regular circuit. The exceptions were trials by special commissions of oyer and terminer and courts-martial. In practice, the special commissions proved to be inconvenient and were used reluctantly. The failure of such a commission in New Jersey revealed some of the difficulties: the single man indicted escaped through the negligence of a "rascally gaoler." The commissioners appointed had either been young, inexperienced lawyers, or laymen with no learning in the law. The sheriff had not collected the witnesses. The court sat without counsel to represent the government and without a clerk. "Thus circumstanced was a court of the highest expectancy ever held in New Jersey."[2]

Everywhere there was a marked reluctance to use the

special commissions. Men appointed as judges showed a noticeable aversion to accepting the commissions.[3] A plea sometimes heard was that the pressure of private business made acceptance impossible.[4] Such an argument had little weight with executive councils who expected men to serve out of "disinterested patriotism and love of justice." [5] Lawyers probably feared that acting as a special commissioner would harm their business. The consensus was that regular justices of the supreme court ought to accept the onerous duty of executing the commissions: "It is Strictly their Office & by Study & Practice they have made themselves Masters of it—Theirs is the Honour, Theirs the Emoluments, and why should they not take whatever may be troublesome or disagreeable therein—" [6] In spite of executive pressure, this disinclination of individuals to serve made the special commissions of oyer and terminer all but useless.

In the greatest crises of the Revolution, a nation dedicated to civil supremacy turned reluctantly to the military for the trial of civilian traitors. In 1777, New York, riddled with disloyalty, threatened by invasion, and without civil courts, ordered the military to bring to trial imprisoned traitors and thus clear its jails. The resolves establishing military jurisdiction set time limits. In relation to rules of evidence and defense counsel, the accused was at a definite disadvantage before these courts. The officers themselves disliked the duty. A group of New York officers reminded the convention that:

State prisoners should and ought to be tryed [sic] by a Court of this State where they should have all the priviledges [sic] of the Law, as Freemen, & that which was once so much boasted of to by the Constitution of Englishmen viz that of Trial by Jurymen of the Vicinity and Council [sic] and further we fear whilst we are struling [sic] for the Sacred Name of Liberty we are establishing the fatal Tendency to Despotism.[7]

The legislators maintained strict surveillance of the military trials. The proceedings were read verbatim before the convention. On occasion the legislators reprimanded officers sharply, and at all times the pardoning power was used generously. When the special resolves expired, the convention put an emphatic period to the court-martial trial of traitors.[8]

The states arrested suspected traitors by a variety of processes. Undoubtedly, temporary injustices were done. Military officers made many arrests, and their authority seems not to have been limited to situations where the militia was in action.[9] Executive and judicial officials at all levels of government, local and county committees, special commissions for detecting conspiracies, judges of supreme courts, and justices of the peace performed this duty.[10] A warrant would be issued in response to an accusation made by an individual citizen. The sheriff would execute it, though sometimes warrants were directed to a militia officer or the Patriot public at large.[11]

In the normal process of commitment, a justice of the peace heard the charges. Evidence was reduced to writing. If it seemed reasonable that the charge could be supported, he committed the accused. Executive councils and special commissions for detecting conspiracies frequently exercised an authority to examine and commit.[12]

In many states the war disrupted the judicial system. Irregularity of court sessions caused long confinement between commitment and trial. This, together with the inadequacy of jails, explains the relatively frequent use of recognizances in treason proceedings. Quite often the accused was given the privilege of finding two sureties for his good behavior and appearance at a future court.[13] The prospect of long confinement also raised the question whether treason was a bailable offense. In a formal opinion, the executive council of one state ruled that justices of the peace could not admit an accused traitor to bail. Rarely were persons committed for treason let to bail.[14]

In Pennsylvania the commitment of a suspected traitor raised the issue of executive interference with an independent judiciary. The supreme executive council confined one Joseph Griswold. Chief Justice Thomas W. McKean issued a writ of habeas corpus to inquire into the causes of commitment. After brief argument, McKean let Griswold to bail. The council charged the justice with acting with undue haste. McKean countered, saying that the writ had been in legal form and that council commitments were no different from those made by justices of the peace. "In my judicial character I am obliged to decide according to the laws and the best of my judgment, un-influenced by any threats or apprehensions of consequences." [15]

Only a small percentage of those arrested and committed on suspicion of treasonable action were ever indicted. Judges, in their charges to grand juries, gave high priority to disloyal activity.[16] Jurors showed a real reticence to expose men to trial for treason. Neither aroused public opinion, nor persuasive attorneys general, could stampede them into finding large numbers of true bills. Again and again, prosecuting attorneys were frustrated by bills returned with the endorsement "ignoramus." [17]

The form and substance of the charge laid in the indictment caused controversy. Generally, several types of treason were included on the assumption that proof of one would warrant conviction.[18] According to English law a specific overt act had to be charged. In Pennsylvania, counsel argued the question of the necessity for detailed description of the overt act in Abraham Carlisle's case. Three treasonable acts had been charged. Though defense counsel argued that the description was too vague, the court upheld the attorney general's contention that practice and precedent required only that the charge be reduced to a "reasonable certainty." [19]

Many American states adopted the English statutory guarantee that the accused be given a copy of the indictment a reasonable time before trial. In Pennsylvania, the courts had been ordered to proceed as in other capital cases. Counsel debated this matter at the 1778 Philadelphia Assize. The court, not regarding itself bound by the letter of the English statute which provided that the accused have the bill ten days before trial, ruled that a minimum of one day was reasonable. In Carlisle's case, defense counsel reopened the question by invoking a provincial statute of 1718 that had adopted English procedural rules. The court stood by its earlier decision. Further, the judges ruled that the prisoner should have a copy of the panel of jurors but not a list of the witnesses.[20]

The extant record contains little information as to process on indictment. A single opinion indicates that English procedure was followed: immediately upon the finding of an indictment, the judge issued a writ of *capias* ordering the sheriff to seize the accused and hold him for trial.[21] Similarly, there is almost no documentary evidence regarding arraignments and pleas to indictments. Undoubtedly, the great majority of accused traitors traversed the indictment in regular form, entering the plea of "not guilty."

The privilege of employing counsel for defense, extended to accused traitors by the Trial of Treasons Act of 1696, was accepted in American practice.[22] The accused often had brilliant counsel. For example, those under indictment at the 1778 Philadelphia Assize were defended by James Wilson, perhaps the foremost lawyer of his day. The record must be regarded as evidence of his ability as well as that of his associates, James Ross and James Lewis. Showing a command of the common law and English and Pennsylvania statutes, they pressed the attorney general to the limit of his resources. In twenty-three cases they won twenty-one acquittals.

Questions related to proper evidence were agitated constantly. At the Philadelphia Assize, several rules emerged. The overt act in the indictment had to be proved before any collateral evidence relative to other acts could be introduced. The court gave the prosecutor a good deal of latitude in the type of evidence it allowed to prove the act charged. For example, one act alleged in the indictment of Carlisle had been holding a commission from Howe to keep the gates of the city. Over defense counsel's objection, testimony that Carlisle had seized goods in his capacity as gatekeeper was admitted by the court as relevant to the charge of accepting a commission.[23]

In John Roberts' case, counsel agitated the question of the quality as evidence of a confession given outside court. Roberts had confessed going to Head of Elk to give information to Robert Galloway, who he knew had joined the British. The court agreed with the defense that such a confession was insufficient evidence to convict. Yet the confession proved the fact of giving intelligence to the enemy, which was then admitted as corroborative evidence to support the charge of aiding the enemy by joining their armies, a treason proved by two other witnesses.[24]

In the case of Joseph Malin, the court held that evidence showing a traitorous intent could not transform an innocent act into a criminal one. Malin had joined an American force, thinking it to be British. The prosecution tried to call a witness to prove that he had intended to join the enemy, but the court refused to admit the evidence. Then the attorney general set out to prove that Malin had been in the armed services of George III in Philadelphia. The indictment specified that adherence had occurred in Chester County. That fact, the court said, needed to be proved before evidence relative to action in another county could be admitted. The prosecution, thus checked on both counts, failed, and the defense won a verdict of "not guilty." [25]

The caution exhibited in these cases cannot be dismissed as mere legal wrangling. Indeed, the cases are eloquent testimony of a desire to dispense justice according to established rules even in time of high political excitement. A jury verdict of "guilty" often brought a motion to arrest judgment.[26] In Carlisle's case, Ross and Wilson argued at length on such a motion. Buttressing their argument with the citation of English and provincial statutes, they tried to convince the court that the indictment was "vague and uncertain," and therefore faulty. The court overruled the motion and gave judgment for the state.[27] In John Roberts' case, counsel moved unsuccessfully for a retrial on the ground that improper evidence had been admitted.[28]

At the time of giving judgment the court informed the accused of the magnitude of the crime. One judge prefaced judgment with this comment:

Treason is a crime of the most dangerous and fatal consequence to society, it is of a most malignant nature; it is of a crimson colour, and of a scarlet dye. Maliciously to deprive one man of life merits death, and blood for blood is just restitution. What punishment then must he deserve, who joins the enemies of his country and endeavours the total destruction of the lives, liberties, and property of all his fellow citizens?

Having counseled the prisoner to spend his last days in prayer, he reminded him of the hideous common law sentence of traitors. He then gave judgment. "You shall be taken back to the place from whence you came, and from thence to the place of execution, and there to be hanged by the neck until dead." [29]

Though a verdict of guilty in a trial of treason traditionally required the death penalty, the states used several alternatives—fines, imprisonment, and other punishments.[30] No state executed a traitor by the common law form. Local legend led several historians to believe that the Frederick

County, Maryland, conspirators suffered the extremities of the old sentence. The justices had given the barbarous old judgment because the legislature had as yet not modified the law. The governor commuted the sentence to simple hanging.[31]

Executive and legislative authorities used their pardoning powers generously. Usually all but the leaders received pardons. Old age, extreme youth, mental incapacity, past conduct, and large families, were advanced as reasons to justify pardons.[32] Some pardons were made conditional upon joining a Patriot military unit.[33] Often pardons were withheld until the accused was in the shadow of the gallows.[34] Officials thought that mercy shown when punishment was imminent would not lessen the force of the example. Frequently, states offered general pardons or "acts of grace." [35] To receive such a pardon a person needed only to take an oath of allegiance to the state. These blanket pardons were based on the assumption that traitorous acts of an accessorial nature resulted from misinformation. When given the facts, an individual would atone for his treason by loyal service to the state.

This liberal use of the pardoning power established a precedent basic to American policy. Those in power have shown a real reticence to execute persons for political crimes, however heinous. A corollary to this aversion has been the tendency to spread the mantle of oblivion over all concerned when the crisis of physical danger is past.

From the viewpoint of the advocate of an extreme policy, the procedure here described exhibits a law of diminishing returns. The policy in regard to traitors became more cautious as the process approached execution. Wholesale arrests and commitments were common. The pace slowed perceptibly at the stage of grand jury indictment. Judges and juries showed great reserve in dealing with the lives of accused traitors. Even after conviction, pardons prevented most executions. Only a tiny minority of those charged with treason ever experienced the terror of the gallows and the hangman's noose. Drastic purges and violent assizes were not a part of the Revolution. There was no reign of terror. The record is one of substantial justice done.

As the law went into action, judges further refined previous statutory definitions of the substantive nature of treason. Reduced to its essence, treason is a treacherous breach of allegiance owed the state. A definition of the crime must consider three factors: the class of persons owing allegiance, the time when allegiance as an obligation enforceable by penalties becomes due, and the actions that constitute a betrayal of allegiance.

Anyone, alien or citizen, permanent resident or visitor, who enjoyed the protection of the government, owed allegiance to the American states. The states followed the broad, long-established English rule.[36] Some men, particularly those of considerable property, claimed a neutral position. They hesitated to take positive action because "it is very uncertain who will Rule yet for the matter is not Determined." [37] State officials rejected the fiction of neutrality. They refused to protect the lives and property of men who shunned the risk of war in the hope of guaranteeing to themselves identification with the victor. They drove men to a decision. John Jay answered one seeking recognition as a neutral: [38]

Sir we have pass'd the Rubicon and it is now necessary [that] every man [should] Take his part, Cast of[f] all allegiance to the King of Great Britain and take an Oath of Alliegance [*sic*] to the States of America or Go over to the Enemy for we have declared ourselves Independent.

The passing of the Rubicon, the Declaration of Independence, made allegiance to American authority a necessary prerequisite to residence in the states. Yet it would have been harsh policy to require that residents owed allegiance on July 4, 1776. Justice demanded that persons be given a reasonable time to decide whether they would become American citizens or remain subjects of George III. The pattern of treason prosecutions indicates that the states permitted a period of election between the Declaration of Independence and the passage of the treason statutes.[39]

The granting of any period of election was an act of grace. Treason might have been committed prior to the passage of statutes defining the crime, and even before independence. Immunity from the obligations of allegiance did not extend to persons who had indicated their attachment to American authority by some positive act. Men serving in the Continental Army owed allegiance to the Continental authority. One justice observed that the governments existing prior to independence derived their power from the sovereign authority of Congress. If a person residing under the protection of these governments tried to destroy them, such an act would amount to treason. Treason, known to the common law as well as the statutes, "might certainly have been committed before the different qualities of the crime were defined, and its punishment declared by positive law." [40] This opinion, however, was obiter dictum. No one was prosecuted under the rule.

Apart from such exceptions, it may be stated generally that allegiance became binding as a legal obligation only with the passage of statutes defining the crime of treason. It was a statutory crime. McKean summed it up when he wrote that "no offence can be adjudged High Treason unless it be clearly and without argument or influence within the meaning of some *Act of Assembly,* for no such act can be extended by Equity." [41]

The actions that constituted a betrayal of allegiance may be grouped in two main classifications: adhering to the enemy, giving him aid and comfort; and levying war against the state. The category of adhering to the enemy was the more comprehensive. The states brought the great majority of traitors to justice as adherents of Great Britain.

Enlistment in the British armed forces was a clear case of adherence. This was the most common treason of the Revolution. Those who recruited men for British service adhered to the enemy. The mere act of remaining in an area occupied by the enemy was not treason.[42] In Carlisle's case, the defense argued that the inhabitants of a conquered city might join the invader. The bonds of allegiance, they said, were dissolved because the state no longer protected its citizens. This argument the court rejected. The state expected its citizens in British-occupied territory to remain passive. Only aid extorted by threats of force could be excused. Any aid given willingly, such as accepting a civil office under the British, amounted to treason.[43]

No clear rule is discernible on the question whether trading with the enemy was treason or a less serious crime. At times the English and Colonial law had regarded such trade as a misdemeanor, at times as treason. The absence of prosecution suggests that the states regarded the action as less than treasonable.[44]

Attempts to give information to the enemy rarely resulted in treason proceedings. Several New York cases arose out of similar and exceptional circumstances. A Whig posed as a British sympathizer and lured Tories into telling him how to get through the American lines to the enemy army.[45] To call such acts treason was an extreme doctrine. The action of the accused men indicated intent only. However disloyal the motive of the men may have been, it is difficult to see how their actions amounted to the treason of adhering to the enemy.[46]

Levying war against the state constituted the second major category of treason during the Revolution. It is not perfectly clear how the states regarded a person who joined the British and fought in their service. The tendency seems to have been to indict such men for levying war and adhering to the enemy. The blending of the two crimes is apparent in the charge against a New Jersey man "committed for High Treason in aiding and assisting the enemy of the United States of America, by taking up Arms against the said States." [47]

The law in action helped to define the words "levying war." The term obviously comprehended activities such as those in which Jacob Rosa was involved. He and his party had been taken in the act of fighting the militia.[48] Military action did not, however, have to come to the point of actual combat to be a levying of war. McKean, following the English rule,[49] gave as his opinion that "Assembling joining and arraying . . . with the forces of the enemy, is a sufficient *overt act,* of levying war." [50]

A new area of constructive treason had been opened when English judges expanded the definition of levying war to include riotous opposition to the enforcement of a general law. The great Virginia draft riots of 1781 resulted in trials for treason. It is difficult to view these men as traitors except under the doctrine of constructive war. There is no proof that they intended to destroy the government of Virginia. Their actions did not arise out of sympathy for Britain. They conceived the draft to be an intolerable burden and prevented the execution of the law. The state pursued a hesitant policy in dealing with the men. They were alternately referred to as traitors and rioters. By charging these rioters with treason, Virginia accepted the constructive English definition of levying war. In the end, though, there was more talk than action. The proceedings against the majority of these "traitors" proved to be abortive.

Legal action further limited the American definition of the crime of treason. Executive and judicial authorities, rejecting theories of constructive treason, restricted the crime to an even narrower range of action. The law moved in the direction of Article 3, section 3 of the federal Constitution.

That traitors should have suffered forfeiture of their estates was a principle in perfect harmony with a contract theory of government. In the famous essay, Locke had written, "the great and chief end, therefore, of men uniting into commonwealths, and putting themselves under government, is the preservation of their property." [51] At the heart of the contract was the obligation of property owners to obey and bear true allegiance to the state. Land ownership, amounting to "tacit" consent, made one a party to the social contract. Any breach of allegiance broke the contract and destroyed the right of the traitor to the protection of his property.

The states effected the forfeiture of the property of persons guilty of treasonable practices by four means: (1) by the inevitable consequence of judgment given in a court of law, (2) by process of outlawry, (3) by special confiscatory statutes, and (4) by bills of attainder.

Probably the most common treason of the Revolution was going over to the enemy. By the nature of the case, one who had gone over to the enemy could not be tried in an ordinary way, nor could he be punished except by confiscation. Such absentees were not beyond the ordinary reach of the law; they could be pursued to an outlawry. At English law, after the finding of a treason indictment, a writ of *capias* was issued; it commanded the sheriff to secure the suspect and hold him for the next assize. If the writ was unenforceable, the suspect was required by proclamation at five successive county courts to surrender. In cases of treason this amounted to a conviction, with resulting attainder and forfeiture.[52]

Eight states made process of outlawry available to enforcement officials: three states adopted the common law in their constitutions, and presumably the process of outlawry with it; [53] five others put outlawry on a statutory basis.[54] In most instances the process was speeded up by shortening the time interval between the original indictment and judgment. Even when altered, outlawry remained complicated and slow. The war had disrupted the judicial systems of many states. Irregularities in proceedings might become the basis of future suits to recover forfeited property. Most states turned to the more direct method of the special confiscatory statute.

The confiscation of property by special statute presented difficult problems. Hard pressed for funds, many state governments regarded the sale of Tory estates as one means of financing the war. The mere seizure of property was a simple matter, but such seizures had to rest on a basis of undoubted legality. Those who purchased the land wanted to be certain of a good title, to be sure that no future legislative or judicial act would invalidate their right.

The two main justifications for confiscation were really the reverse sides of the same coin and depended on the attitude toward allegiance. Some states permitted the claim of absentee Tories to British citizenship to stand.[55] Here the justification of forfeiture was the clearly established right of a government to dispose of an enemy alien's property.[56] Other states evaded the issue of allegiance, referring to the Tories simply as inhabitants, or property owners.[57] Three states claimed the allegiance of persons affected by their confiscation statutes.[58] Thus eight states, either explicitly or implicitly, based their confiscatory action in the law of treason.

The process established by these laws varied from summary executive action to well-regulated procedure before courts of law. Most drastic was the Pennsylvania law; the supreme executive council simply ordered suspects to return for trial. Failure to return within forty days brought automatic condemnation. In New York, a grand jury found a bill against the absentee. The bill was returned to the supreme court of judicature. Failure to traverse the indictment brought condemnation. Delaware confiscated property of named absentees who failed to return and abjure their oath to George III. South Carolina sequestered property, putting it in the hands of commissioners until such time as the accused returned to clear himself in court. North Carolinian absentees had to clear themselves before the general court. In Connecticut and New Jersey, a jury verdict finding that a person had adhered to the enemy by leaving the state brought condemnation. Massachusetts and Rhode Island began process by a complaint to a justice of an inferior court. The sheriff exhibited notices of action at two successive county courts and at such time a jury tried the issue. The judgment rendered was civil, effecting confiscation only.[59]

State officials used the powers granted in these laws extensively. For example, over a three-year period the Pennsylvania executive proclaimed 488 persons. It is now possible to account for 380 who were attainted without trial because of failure to return. Of those who surrendered within the specified time, the council discharged seventy-one. All had a regular trial. The grand jury failed to indict two, and fourteen won acquittals. Fourteen were convicted, one after two and one-half years.[60] In New York, grand jury indictments were based on the depositions of two witnesses. The bill, in each case, was specific, and proof was demanded that he not only went behind enemy lines, but also aided the enemy. From February, 1780 to December, 1783, the state won 825 convictions. Most of the indictments originated in the counties of Westchester, Albany, and Tryon. The majority of those attainted were yeomen farmers.[61]

Maryland, proceeding only in clear-cut cases of betrayal, brought her absentee traitors to justice by an accelerated process of outlawry. Five Somerset men who had participated in a British maritime raid were condemned by the general court one year after the sheriff had returned the *capias* endorsed *non est inventus*. At the spring term for the Eastern shore in 1780, the state concluded outlawry proceedings against several men who had joined Howe's army during the Philadelphia campaign of 1777–78.[62] In New Jersey, special commissioners made returns to the justices of the peace naming those persons who, having left the state, were guilty of treasonable practices. The justice impaneled a jury to determine the facts of the case, and the effects of an "inquisition found" were similar to an indictment. The sheriff made proclamation, ordering the accused to traverse the inquisition. Six hundred and seventy-five persons were proclaimed. It is no longer possible to determine precisely how many cases were brought to judgment.[63]

The remaining method by which absentees could be brought to account was by bills of attainder. Such bills were in effect confiscatory statutes since there was little likelihood that a person attainted in this manner would make himself available to undergo the full rigor of the treason sentence. For practical purposes, the bills of attainder prescribed forfeiture as the punishment of the attainted.

The states used two types of bills of attainder, absolute and conditional. The absolute type made no provision for trial in the law courts. The conditional bills decreed persons to be guilty of the crime described in the statute, but provided a period of time during which they might come in and stand trial. If they failed to surrender within the time period, the attainder would operate.[64] Four states used absolute [65] and four used conditional bills of attainder.[66]

Problems of allegiance explain in part why the states resorted to bills of attainder. Operating through this medium, the legislators did not have to be concerned with fine-spun legal distinctions involving citizenship. In the bills of attainder they dispensed quick justice, making the rules as they proceeded. Bills of attainder need no legal justification for they are laws unto themselves, "being for all intents and purposes new laws made *pro re nata,* and by no means an execution of such as are already in being." [67] Beyond the confines of narrow legalism, however, it is difficult to justify such bills. The prohibition of bills of attainder in the Constitution of the United States had its precedent in the Revolution. During the war, opinion ran strongly against the device. The constitutions of Maryland and Massachusetts contained outright prohibitions.[68] The New York Constitution of 1777 permitted bills of attainder for the duration of the war, but such acts were to work no corruption of the blood.[69]

The fact that the states used bills of attainder, in spite of the growing opinion that they were unjust, illustrates the depth of the feeling against the old official class. Most of these laws sorted out persons of a bad pre-eminence, from the Patriot point of view, as objects of vengeance. Royal governors, councilors, and other crown officials were favorite targets in the attainders.

The incompatibility of bills of attainder with American concepts of criminal justice is well illustrated by the case of Josiah Phillips and the New York attainder of 1779. Phillips was a Virginia brigand who mixed treason with plundering. With a price on his head, the marauder showed amazing skill in avoiding capture. The legislature condemned him as a traitor by bill of attainder, giving him a period of time in which to surrender and stand trial. Phillips, captured after the expiration of the time period, was, by the bill, already a condemned man. Yet, the attorney general, Edward Randolph, began proceedings against the outlaw at common law. He was indicted, tried, sentenced, and hanged. The clear implication was that Randolph thought the judges would regard a bill of attainder as contrary to the fundamental law of Virginia, and unenforceable.[70]

The New York bill of attainder, after a stormy career

in three sessions of the legislature, passed in 1779. The bill, hotly debated then, has been condemned ever since. It has been charged that the legislators were moved by a desire for personal and political revenge, by religious animosity, and by cupidity. A close examination of the evidence leads to the conclusion that such charges were, at best, half-truths. Contemporary criticism of revision made in the New York Senate and Council was more valid. Senators and councilors protested it as unjust and inexpedient. In addition to inviting retaliation, the bill violated the separation of powers, ran roughshod over rules of evidence, denied trial by jury, and put persons condemned in double jeopardy. The bill openly flouted tradition and showed how ill-adapted the legislative process is to exact criminal justice. It was an exception to the tendency of the times, which was to prohibit bills of attainder. Contemporaries, Patriots as well as Tories, condemned it.[71]

The question of the "justice" of the forfeitures is, for the historian, unanswerable. Revolutionary settlements work great hardship on property owners who try to maintain neutrality or who choose the losing side. None of the statutes were passed in a vacuum. Personal pique, politics, and class animosity doubtless influenced decisions. Nevertheless, underlying these laws was the common principle that the validity of one's title to property depended on loyalty to the state. Such a policy was certainly no revolution-born innovation. These statutes created the dilemma of the Tory landowner. He could become an enemy alien or a traitor. Either way he lost his property.

6

The Constitutional Definition and First Application

The question of treason quickly came before the Philadelphia convention, bringing with it the further questions of sovereignty and resistance. All agreed that a definition of the high crime should be a part of the fundamental law. With this assumption, agreement ended. Both the New Jersey and the Pinckney plans would have empowered Congress to define treason.[1] These suggestions then went to the committee on detail. There a working definition was stated. In one important particular the committee altered the original proposals. Definition of the crime was not to be left to the legislature, but was to be limited by the Constitution itself. The committee formula contained the main elements of the final definition: that treason should consist of levying war against, or adhering to the enemies of, the United States or any of them; two witnesses were required; any forfeiture or corruption of the blood was to be limited to the lifetime of the convicted.[2]

In debate, the committee of the whole agitated these questions: was the power to punish treason an exclusive power of the federal government; was the definition too loose or too narrow; were the guarantees concerning evidence adequate?

The question whether the power to punish treason was

to be exercised exclusively by the central government went squarely to the question of sovereignty. Clearly the punishment of a breach of allegiance was the act of the sovereign. Several members insisted that sovereignty was indivisible, and that the power to punish treason should be vested solely in the federal government.[3] One raised the question of an insurrection such as Bacon's Rebellion, arguing that in the new jurisdiction this would amount to treason against a state; another thought that such action would be treason against the United States.[4] Madison appears to have stated the consensus: ". . . the definition here was of treason against *the* U. S. it would seem that the individual states wd. be left in possession of a concurrent power. . . ."[5] Sherman suggested that the practical line between sovereignties would be determined by the nature of the resistance. Opposition to state law would be treason against the part; resistance to the general law would constitute the crime against the whole.[6] In the absence of a specific prohibition, it must be concluded that the intention was that the sovereign power of punishing a breach of allegiance would be exercised concurrently.

The *Journal* is silent on the question of conflict of allegiance. At a later date, Luther Martin stated that he proposed an amendment.[7] Prophetically he noted that circumstances might pose a dilemma for the citizen owing a dual allegiance. In the event of state-federal conflict, which sovereign should be defied? Martin favored the state, with the provision that, if war be levied by the state against the nation, the conduct of the parties should "be regulated by the *laws of war* and of *nations.*" He hit home when he said:

By the *principles* of the American revolution, *arbitrary power may* and *ought* to be resisted, even by *arms* if necessary. The time may come, when it shall be the *duty* of a *State,* in order to preserve itself from the oppression of the general government, to have recourse to the sword. . . .

But this was protest. The clear intent of the Constitution was to make the federal sovereignty supreme in the event of a conflict of allegiance. Could it have been otherwise? There can be no right of unsuccessful armed resistance.

The statute of Edward III had been definitive of the common law, restrictive in its influence. The Convention debated whether their definition was sufficiently precise or too rigid. Madison argued that the proposed definition was inflexible; he would have left Congress with a power to expand or contract the specifications of the crime as circumstances might dictate.[8] The discussion went against him, the members favoring adherence to the ancient statute.[9] Whether their intent was to admit the English case law that had expanded the meaning of the old act remains a mystery. Here, Mr. King, putting his finger on future reality, "observed that the controversy relative to Treason might be of less magnitude than was supposed as the legislature might punish capitally under other names than Treason." [10]

On the procedural side, the fathers were razor-sharp. John Dickinson wanted to know the meaning of the requirement of the "testimony of two witnesses." Did they have to testify to the same overt act, or different overt acts? He thought the proof of an overt act essential. Franklin spoke to this, desiring two witnesses to the same overt act; ". . . prosecutions for treason were generally virulent; and perjury too easily made use of against innocence." [11] The precise requirement concerning evidence carried as an amendment by a vote of eight to three.

Article III, section 3 read:

Treason against the United States shall consist only in levying war against them, or in adhering to their enemies, giving them aid and comfort. No person shall be convicted of treason unless on the testimony of two witnesses to the same overt act, or on confession in open court.

The Congress shall have the power to declare the punishment of treason, but no attainder of treason shall work corruption of the blood or forfeiture except during the life of the person attainted.

The question of the soundness of the treason definition appeared infrequently in the ratification debates. Luther Martin attacked the provision as an assault on states' rights.[12] Wilson and Madison defended it as a limitation of the law and a guarantee of personal right. In *The Federalist* Number 43, Madison argued that factions inevitably attended free government. Such parties "usually wreaked their alternate malignity on each other" by creating "new-fangled and artificial treasons." [13]

The Convention and Congress made a few further procedural refinements. The Convention debated the question whether the presidential power of pardon ought to extend to cases of treason. Randolph thought not: "The president may himself be guilty. The traytors [*sic*] may be his own instruments." Several proposals came forth to vest the power in the legislature or to have it shared by president and senate. Wilson, arguing against the motion, noted that the president was impeachable. King thought this power inappropriate for the legislature. With obvious reference to Shays's Rebellion, he said that one legislature would have pardoned them all, the next would have hanged them all.[14]

In 1790, Congress provided that the penalty for treason would be death by hanging. The same law adopted most of the procedural guarantees of the Trial of Treasons Act: The accused was to have a copy of the indictment and a list of the witnesses and jurors at least three days before trial; he was to have counsel and compulsory process; he could peremptorily challenge thirty-five of the jury panel. The act of standing mute was to be regarded as a proper plea of "not guilty." [15]

During the administrations of Washington and Adams, the treason law was twice applied. In both cases the resistance was to the tax laws. Both risings occurred in Pennsylvania. In each instance the resistance came to be associated with the emerging political opposition to the Federalists. The story of the Whiskey Rebellion has been well told.[16] Hamilton's excise, levied on the distillery, was an integral and important part of his financial scheme. Opposition to such laws was no new phenomenon in western Pennsylvania. Resistance, beginning with petitions and resolutions, soon proceeded to tar and feathers and other acts of violence that recurred sporadically through 1792 and 1793. The law went unenforced, for the most part.

A major objection to the original law had been that all trials were to be held in Philadelphia. In April, 1794, Hamilton sponsored an amendment giving jurisdiction to the state courts. At the same time he instituted process against noncomplying distillers, but he did this under the old law. It is difficult to escape the conclusion that Hamilton both expected and wanted resistance. The contemporary charge was that he wanted to demonstrate the need for a standing army.

In June, the marshal went out to serve the warrants. This attempt triggered the insurrection. It began with an attack on Bower Hill, the mansion of the collector, John Neville. He repulsed the first attack and sent to Pittsburgh for aid. About a dozen regular soldiers were sent to Bower Hill. The militia, anti-excise almost to a man, met at nearby Couch's Fort and decided to renew the attack. Next day a small battle was waged and Bower Hill sacked.

After Bower Hill, the plot thickened. The mass was ready to be led to more desperate measures; indeed, they sometimes pushed their leaders. The appeal to arms revealed internal stresses. Men of substance, some of whom had been anti-excise, scrambled to disassociate themselves. Moderates, of whom the lawyer Hugh M. Brackenridge was most conspicuous, participated in subsequent events to divert the resistance into less-violent courses. Brackenridge was perfectly aware that he walked a narrow path between treason and mob retaliation. The Bower Hill rioters met at Mingo Creek to consider what to do next. Brackenridge attended, attempted to moderate, and reminded the crowd that their action was proceeding to treason. A stormy session produced the decision to call a general muster of the militia at Braddock's Field outside Pittsburgh. The Monongahela country stood on the verge of all-out resistance and class war. Prosperous Pittsburghers buried their valuables, fearing the worst if the hill people got loose in "Sodom." More than 5,000 men gathered at Braddock's Field. It was a riotous day, punctuated by the steady fire of small arms. Brackenridge and other moderates skillfully diverted the proposal to assault the federal fort at Pittsburgh. The affair ended with a tense parade through the city.

Early in August, the Washington administration was ready to act. Hamilton prepared the way: on August 2 he wrote to Washington, "The opposition had continued and matured, till it has at length broken out in acts which are presumed to amount to treason." [17] Attorney General William Bradford had furnished an opinion, the first to bring in the English doctrine of constructive war. He had no trouble finding, in the English elementary writers, the dictum that forcible resistance to the enforcement of a general law amounted to treason. Further, he thought that no marshal's posse could restore order. He advised calling out the militia.[18] On the same day, Washington called a meeting of federal and state officials. The decision was made to use military force. Within the week, Justice James Wilson certified that process of justice had collapsed; Hamilton turned in a long report; Washington, in a proclamation, announced his opinion that the resistance had been treasonable. The call went out for 13,000 militia.

With club in one hand, the government held out an olive branch in the other. Five commissioners were sent west to attempt to settle the trouble. The commissioners were empowered to accept individual submissions for a period of about two weeks. After some wrangling, a west country committee recommended submission and the process began, though acceptance was by no means unanimous. With submission went the promise of amnesty and future pardon. But, the militia was already in motion. Hamilton, preaching coercion, had his way. The army mustered at Carlisle. Washington went out for a brief tour of inspection, and the decision was made to move west. News of the army's coming sped across the mountains. Most of the leaders of the rising fled the country. The army came on, meeting no opposition. The moderates passed nervous days as the interrogations proceeded. Hamilton himself quizzed Brackenridge. The lawyer was so unsure of himself that he had already drafted a brief of his defense should he be charged with treason. The army rounded up suspects, being none too gentle in the process. Most of those taken had played insignificant roles. Inevitably, there were examples of brutality. In the end, twenty prisoners were marched back across the mountains, arriving in Philadelphia on Christmas Day.

The trials were held at the spring circuit of the Philadelphia circuit court; they dragged on until November. Most of the men in custody had played minor roles. The district attorney sent thirty-five bills for treason to the grand jury. Eleven were returned, endorsed *ignoramus*. Of the twenty-four men indicted, thirteen had fled.[19] The defense led off with a general procedural protest. The venire had been incorrectly summoned; counsel had not been given the caption of the indictments, nor the addresses of the jurors and witnesses. Judge Peters delayed proceedings for three days so that the statute might be complied with. Court and counsel labored under considerable difficulty. Some cases were carried over to the next term because of the absence of witnesses.[20] In one instance, the court found that the wrong man had been apprehended! After months of confinement, he was released immediately.[21]

The government obtained convictions in two cases. The first involved one Philip Vigol.[22] A man of small consequence, he had participated actively in the destruction of a collector's house immediately after the Bower Hill riot. Both defense and prosecution accepted without question the English doctrine of a constructive levying of war. The case turned on evidence, that is, whether there were two witnesses to an overt act. There were. Paterson's charge to the jury was sharp and decisive; to him, the evidence and intent were unquestionable. Taken together, "the crime of High Treason is consummate in the contemplation of the Constitution and law of the United States."

The second conviction came in the case of John Mitchell.[23] He had taken active part in the meeting at Couch's Fort, the attack on Neville's house, and the muster at Braddock's Field. At the last, in an advanced state of intoxication, he had vociferously condemned the government. Again the major issue was evidence: four witnesses had seen him at Couch's. One had seen him at Neville's, though another said that "it ran in his head that he had seen him there." One testified to his attendance at Braddock's Field and Mitchell had confessed to that. The real question was whether the meeting at the fort and the attack on Bower Hill had been a continuous event. If so, the two-witness requirement was satisfied.

Again the district attorney unhesitatingly turned to English law. Levying war "must be the same in technical interpretation, whether committed under a republican or regal form of government." He found two unequivocal rules in the books: to force the repeal of a statute, to prevent the execution of a public law, or to suppress the officers of government amounted to levying war. Further, in treason all are principals. He cited the commentaries from Coke to Blackstone and threw in two cases for good measure.

The defense contested both law and evidence. Though admitting that Mitchell's acts were criminal, the defense contended that they did not amount to treason. They posted a warning lest every "riot [be] aggravated into high treason." Counsel argued that the penal code covered the action; resistance to process was a misdemeanor. Turning to the English books, they tried to establish the rule that in cases of constructive war the intent had to be to suppress *all* conventicles, brothels, and so on. This was patently not a correct reading. Examining the evidence, they insisted that each act alleged must stand separately. The two-witness requirement had been met only in the Couch's Fort incident. This they argued, was not treason, but a mere conspiracy to levy war.

Paterson gave the argument short shrift. Applying the English rule of constructive treason, he stated that war had been levied. The incidents alleged could be considered as a continuous act. One observer thought that the defense had lost the case when the jury had been selected. The young, inexperienced attorney had rejected western jurors and accepted twelve Quakers "on the supposition that Quakers would condemn no person to death; but he was utterly mistaken." The commentator continued, "choose a jury of Quakers in all common cases such as murder, rape and so forth . . . but in every possible case of insurrection, rebellion and treason, give him Presbyterians on the jury." [24] The Quakers convicted.

There was a reluctance to push the law to the extremity of execution. Albert Gallatin spoke truth: "But he is certainly an object of pity more than of punishment . . . for he is a rough ignorant German who knew very well he was committing a riot and he ought to have been punished for it, but who had certainly no idea it amounted to levying war and high treason. . . ." [25] Washington agreed, and issued pardons. In fact, the last official act of his presidency was to grant amnesty to the "rebels" who had fled.[26]

To the Federalists, the Whiskey Insurrection was the inevitable result of the machinations of the Democratic societies. The Federalists thought criticism of government to be disloyal, the harbinger of treason. Through the following years, the course of foreign affairs confirmed their fears. As the nation proceeded from crisis to crisis, opposition mounted. The cold war with France created the opportunity for repression. In the context of undeclared war, the Federalists saw a chance to destroy the emerging party of opposition. By statute, they strove to bring in that part of the criminal law of England that made political resistance a crime. The original Sedition Act, in addition to establishing the crimes of seditious libel and conspiracy to oppose government, had declared France an enemy and applied the treason law. Though the last provision failed of passage, the Federalists persisted in their efforts to root out political opposition by applying the criminal law.[27]

No complex theory of conspiracy is needed to explain the house tax rebellion of the spring of 1798.[28] Its causes were spontaneous and indigenous to the northeastern counties of Pennsylvania. The German farmers there were politically alert. The solvent of Republicanism, poured through the funnel of the *Aurora,* had worked powerfully to dissolve their Federalism and make the farmers verbally Jeffersonian. These yeomen were thrifty to the point of penuriousness; they hated taxation in any form. Even the weather contributed; a late spring delayed plowing and the men were available for mischief.

The tax fell on land, slaves, and dwellings. Assessment of the dwelling rates caused the trouble. The number and size of windows were used as a rough rule to determine total value. As the assessors moved about measuring the windows, the notion developed that the glass, not the building, was being taxed. When the assessors came into northeastern Pennsylvania they ran into real trouble. Everywhere the farmers uttered threats of violence. One assessor suffered the indignity of being soaked with scalding water poured down on him by the hostile dame of the house. The *Aurora* took up the incident and dubbed it the "hot water war." [29] Prudently, the assessors fell back to Quakerstown to regroup. They decided to try again, working together in twos and threes.

They reappeared at Milford and there ran into John Fries. He was a likeable, loquacious, German auctioneer. Finding the assessors at dinner, he warned them to desist. They persisted. The temper of the countryside was indicated in a tavern meeting where "they damned the house-tax and stamp act . . . they damned the alien and sedition law, and finally all the laws . . . They damned the Constitution . . . They damned the Congress, and damned the President. . . ." [30] In addition to all this "damning," there was some mistreatment of the assessors, and they retreated again to Quakerstown.

The crisis came when a federal marshal moved into the county to execute warrants directed against those who had resisted the tax. He met with resentment, but no violence, as he began gathering his prisoners at Bethlehem. On March 6, the marshal obtained information that an attempt would be made to rescue the prisoners. He immediately summoned the posse; a dozen or more men responded and mounted guard outside the tavern where the prisoners had been located.

The countryside was literally up in arms. On the night of March 6, Fries and others gathered at a tavern and agreed to an association, the object of which was to effect the release of the prisoners. On the morning of the seventh, several groups took the road to Bethlehem. Two armed men arrived prematurely. When asked about their business, they responded that "they came out on a shooting frolic." Questioned further about what the target would be, they said they did not know.

The marshal, thinking the mob would arrive in small groups, sent men to stop them at a convenient bridge. While the marshal's men were trying to dissuade such a group, Fries arrived and assumed command. There was an altercation about the bridge toll but Fries resolved this, and the little army moved on toward Bethlehem. They were a sight to behold. First came a uniformed troop of horse, then two companies of infantry led by Fries with drawn sword. They sported tricolor cockades in their hats. The cavalry drew up before the tavern while the infantry, in a single file, marched twice around the tavern and then drew up in ranks. There was some huzzaing. The force numbered over one hundred, though the crowd around the building was estimated to be as high as five hundred.

Fries parleyed with the marshal who refused to release the prisoners. Outside the tavern again, Fries harangued the troops. An attack was in order, but he commanded his men not to fire first. Expecting to be the first to fall, he told his men to take care of themselves. "Slay, strike, or do as well as you can." It never came to this. The marshal released the prisoners on their promise to surrender themselves at Philadelphia. Convinced that the men had been delivered, the army marched home again.

Within five days of the Bethlehem Riot, the Adams administration acted. A Presidential Proclamation commanded the insurgents to disband. It announced that the crimes committed amounted to treason and contained no amnesty nor promise of pardon.[31] Simultaneously, the president requested Governor Mifflin to call five troops of militia. Mifflin responded immediately, though an unsuccessful attempt was made to block the move in the Pennsylvania legislature. The command went to Brigadier General William Macpherson, commandant of a crack corps of Philadelphia cavalry. Macpherson heralded his coming with a German-language proclamation in which he explained the excise law and the criminality of the opposition.[32]

The army met no resistance. Inevitably charges of cruelty and abuse of authority were hurled at the troops. The Reading *Adler* and the *Aurora* screamed the accusation. In due course the suspects were rounded up. The troops found Fries conducting an auction. He fled, but was soon captured.

The trials came on at the federal circuit court in Philadelphia at the spring term, 1799. From the beginning, the rule *stare decisis* laid its hand on the proceedings. In charging the grand jury, Iredell stated that the application of force with intent to prevent the execution of a congressional law amounted to levying war. He saw the cause of the insurrection in the continuous attack on government in the Republican press.[33]

The indictment alleged the Bethlehem rising as the overt act. A motion to have the trials moved to Northampton County was unsuccessfully advanced by the defense. Sitgreaves opened for the government; he stated the law generally and previewed the evidence. The evidence was very full, far exceeding the two-witness requirement.[34] It included a confession made by Fries early in April in which he had stated that he had gone to Bethlehem not to effect the rescue, but for personal reasons. He said his action "proceeded from a general aversion to the law, and an intention to impede and prevent its execution." [35] Rawle then spoke for the government, furnishing the American and English precedents.

Dallas, Ewing, and Lewis defended Fries. Though they had a weak case, they argued with ingenuity. They drew a pathetic picture of Fries, arguing that he labored under great disadvantage. Public opinion was aroused against him; the jury was not of the vicinage. Relative to the law, they argued that Fries's action did not add up to treason. The *quo animo* was not there. At most the affair was a riot or a misdemeanor under the Sedition Act. In any event, they asked, why go to the English books for a definition of American law? Lewis, though, did go to that law and attempted to extract from the *Case of Lord George Gordon* the rule that only resistance to the militia law could amount to treason. The defense was imaginative. They suggested that Adams' proclamation amounted to a pardon; they reminded the jurors that in the recent English cases involving Hardy, Tooke, and Gordon the juries had refused to convict. They tried the rule of reasonable doubt, "for, if you doubt . . . you must acquit." [36]

Rawle, for the government, rebutted these arguments with skill. The burden of his argument went to the point that "what, then, in England is called a constructive levying of war, in this country must be called direct levying of war."

The judges charged the jury separately, but the message was the same. They reviewed the appropriate American and English precedent and restated the law. The action was not riot, nor rescue, nor conspiracy. The combination of force and intent amounted to levying war.[37]

The jury was back directly with a verdict of guilty. It had been a long, fatiguing trial, but the defense persisted. Lewis, alleging that a juror had prejudged Fries, moved for a new trial. After lengthy argument, the court reluctantly granted the motion.[38]

The second trial was held before the same court. Samuel Chase presided. That this notorious spring circuit did not turn out to be a "bloody assize" certainly was not his fault. Fries had been arraigned on his indictment, and counsel were entering the court, when Chase handed down several papers from the bench. Lewis, again assigned to defend Fries, began to read. He was not far into the text when he threw the papers down and in a state of agitation announced that he would not defend Fries. The paper contained Chase's statement of the law of treason and had been delivered before argument. Chase and Peters tried to convince Lewis to proceed. They pointed out that the calendar was very full and that the law was clear. Lewis refused. The court adjourned. Next day Chase literally pleaded with Lewis. The paper had been withdrawn; Lewis might conduct his argument as he saw fit. Lewis persisted in his refusal, announcing that he would have no part of a prejudged trial.[39] It is also possible that he thought his course was in Fries's interest. To fortify the impression of arbitrary proceedings might influence ultimate executive clemency. Chase, out of patience, announced that he would act as prisoner's counsel and that justice would be done. A bewildered Fries accepted the offer. The district attorney, embarrassed by the circumstances, made a brief, simple statement of the law.[40] The evidence was much the same as at the first trial. Chase, charging the jury, stated the law as Iredell and Peters had previously.[41] The verdict was guilty. Fries was given an opportunity to arrest judgment. Before giving judgment, Chase delivered a lecture calculated to horrify the convicted man.[42]

The Fries trial obviously had not occurred in a vacuum. McKean's sweeping victory in the Pennsylvania election of 1799 measured the surge of the Republican tide. To all good Federalists, Pennsylvania was a sink of political sin. The settled policy of the high Federalists was to use the criminal law to root out opposition; and where better than in Pennsylvania. Hamilton and his coterie in the Adams' Cabinet had pushed the prosecution vigorously. Having brought Fries to book, they now pushed him on toward the gallows.

Adams was in Massachusetts at the time of the verdict in the first trial. To him, the Cabinet directed a stream of correspondence that moved all in one direction. Pickering wrote of the need to vindicate the law, particularly in Pennsylvania: a horrible example was a public necessity; "And painful as is the idea of taking the life of a man, I feel a calm and solid satisfaction that an opportunity is now presented, in executing the just sentence of the law. . . ." [43] Wolcott, Hamilton's spokesman, expressed similar sentiments.[44] But Adams was not to be stampeded. Within the week letters came from Quincy indicating the President's reservations. He inquired of the attorney general what defense Lewis had made.[45] He asked the secretary of state about Fries's character and the scope of the rising. The decision, he wrote, would "prove a severe trial to my heart" for "neither humanity nor public justice must be violated." [46]

Adams' decision was postponed by Lewis' successful motion for a new trial. The motion was granted, Pickering wrote, "To the surprise and chagrin of many." [47] During the summer, petitions for mercy came to Adams. Since any pardon could have been pleaded at bar at a new trial, the Cabinet pressed the President to resist the appeals. Lee wrote that "mercy to few is cruelty to many." [48]

The Cabinet met immediately after the second conviction of Fries. The members agreed unanimously that the execution should not be delayed. Lee and Stoddard thought that Fries at the end of a rope would be sufficient example. Wolcott was of a mind to hang them all. Again they pressed Adams.[49] The President answered quickly and with simple dignity. In disagreeing with his Cabinet, he assumed full responsibility for "one more appeal to the humane and generous nature of the American people." He ordered the attorney general to prepare the pardons for his signature.[50] Whether Adams was moved by mercy or acted to arrest a miscarriage of justice cannot be known. In all probability his motives were mixed, but one thing is certain. The President knew that pardon would drive deeper the wedge splitting the Federalist party. The pardon and the appointment of the Murray mission to France were the acts of a stubbornly independent man whose sense of right would not yield to party pressure.

The pardon was immediately injected into politics.[51] In his famous assault on Adams, Hamilton cited the pardon as evidence to prove the President's duplicity and weakness.[52] For nine years Adams made no answer. Then he wrote that he had assumed full responsibility before the American people. The pardon would, he said, "console me in my last hour."[53] John Adams' epitaph might well be amended to read, "Here lies John Adams who made peace with France in 1800, and pardoned John Fries."

In the state trials resulting from the two Pennsylvania insurrections, Federalist judges greatly expanded the scope of the crime of levying war. The tendency in the federal jurisdiction was to veer away from the adoption of substantive common law crimes. The interpretation of the law of treason by Iredell, Peters, Patterson, and Chase must be seen as an exception to this tendency. They brought in the doctrine of a constructive levying of war, and it remains good law to this day.

7

John Marshall and the Law of Treason

When Aaron Burr's term as vice-president ended in March,
1805, the door to political preferment slammed in the face
of an ambitious man. To many Federalists he appeared as
Hamilton's murderer; Republicans saw him as the would-be
betrayer of Jefferson. So circumstanced, Burr turned to his
western enterprise.

Burr wove a tangled web, one that only recently has been
entirely visible.[1] At various times, one or more of the following alternatives were strands of that web: the severing of the
entire trans-Appalachian west from the Union; a filibustering raid into Spanish territory; settlement of lands in the
Washita Valley. The conspirator, sometimes subtly, sometimes brazenly, seemed to move in all directions at once.
Seeking foreign aid, he contacted the ministers of Great
Britain and Spain. Probing for areas of domestic discontent,
he revealed himself to officers of the army and navy. Through
the West he sought out persons of power, the Morgans of
Pennsylvania, Andrew Jackson. He fished in the troubled
waters of New Orleans politics. The key to all, though, was
despicable General James Wilkinson. The realization of any
of the major aims of the conspiracy depended upon the
capacity and willingness of Wilkinson to trigger a war along

the uneasy Spanish-American frontier. The conspiracy was formidable and, without doubt, treasonable.

In the summer of 1806, Burr launched the grand expedition. Two confederates, Samuel Swartout and Erick Bollman, went ahead with reassuring letters addressed to Wilkinson. Burr proceeded to the point of rendezvous, the idyllic island retreat of Harman Blennerhassett, in the Ohio River. The impressionable Irishman fell to the task with vigor. He let contracts at Marietta for boats and supplies. The island bustled as men assembled and gathered supplies. With things proceeding on schedule, Burr went to Nashville to buy more boats. While there he completed the transaction for the Washita lands.

Jefferson, informed of the conspiracy, sent a special agent to investigate. The agent alerted Governor Edward Tiffin of Ohio. The governor called out his militia and seized the boats at Marietta. Jefferson moved again, this time in response to a letter from Wilkinson who had decided to abandon Burr. A Presidential Proclamation warned all citizens to stay clear of the enterprise. Receipt of the proclamation put the Virginia militia in motion.

Blennerhassett, threatened by the militia on two sides, decided to move the expedition. Hastily, boats passed back and forth from the Ohio shore. The men worked round the clock, loading supplies and casting bullets by the light of bonfires. Virtually at the moment of departure, the single act of violence associated with the conspiracy occurred: A Mr. Tupper grabbed Blennerhassett and announced loudly that he was arrested "in the name of the commonwealth." Instantly Tupper stood in a ring of rifles. One of the party said flatly that he would "lieve as not shoot Tupper." Tupper released Blennerhassett and the expedition departed. Twenty men, already fugitives, floated south down the Ohio in three boats. This was the overt act of levying war for which Burr was later indicted.[2]

Burr joined the party at the mouth of the Cumberland. The army, now swollen to one hundred men, floated serenely down the Mississippi. Meanwhile, Wilkinson stepped up the pace. By concluding an agreement with Spain, he averted war along the Sabine. Then he played the role of "saviour of his country" to the hilt, crying alarm in every direction. He arrested Bollman and Swartout and sent them north. The army stopped Burr at Bayou Pierre and packed him off to the east for trial.

The initiative was Jefferson's. In his annual message he had spoken generally of the conspiracy; he neither hinted treason nor mentioned Burr. The House of Representatives, driven by John Randolph, passed two resolutions calling for more information. The President, in possession of a vague letter from Wilkinson, responded in a special message. Evidence, said Jefferson, was confused and shot through with rumor. One incontestable fact emerged, the identity "of the principal actor, whose guilt is placed beyond question." Aaron Burr was named as that actor. Burr's purpose, Jefferson charged, had been "the severance of the Union of those States beyond the Alleghany [*sic*] mountains." The President had committed himself to the prosecution of Burr.[3]

The capital seethed with rumor. On the day of the special message, Bollman and Swartout arrived under military guard, flesh-and-blood evidence of the plot. Next morning, the administration moved in the Senate. In closed session, Jefferson's spokesman, William B. Giles, introduced a bill to suspend the writ of habeas corpus. The senators, with only a single dissenting vote, rushed the bill through three readings in a single day. Assured that the writ would be suspended, Jefferson instructed the district attorney to move for a warrant against Bollman and Swartout. Only after the writ had been suspended would he permit their release from military custody. But Giles's bill was not law. The House did not consider the bill Friday, the day of Senate passage. The House met in secret session on Monday. After hearing the bill, they opened the doors. Congressman after congressman rose to write his sentiments into the record. The bill failed, 113 to 19.[4]

On the same day, attorneys for Bollman and Swartout applied to Circuit Court Judge William Cranch for a writ of habeas corpus. The court took the prisoners on a bench warrant charging them with treason. The defense moved for discharge, and the court asked for evidence to justify continuing the commitment. A large crowd pressed into the court on Wednesday. The attorney general produced two affidavits by Wilkinson and a deposition by Eaton as evidence. The three-man court divided: two Republican judges thought the evidence adequate to commit; the lone Federalist disagreed.[5]

Immediately, defense counsel applied to the Supreme Court for writs of habeas corpus and *certiorari*. After some argument as to the competence of the justices *en banc* to issue a habeas corpus, John Marshall ruled that the writ could be issued. The marshal returned that he held the prisoners by order of the circuit court. Then the defense moved that the prisoners be discharged or admitted to bail. The evidence did not show probable cause. Taking a passing shot at Jefferson, Henry Lee said, ". . . no hearsay, no opinion of any person, however high in office . . . can be received in this examination." The defense concluded that the evidence showed no overt act nor any treasonable intent.[6]

Caesar Rodney presented the government's case. Rodney and his associates were on thin ice, and they knew it. Going to common law, they argued generally: "in treason all are principals"; the doctrine of constructive war was applicable, ". . . if the constituted authorities of the United States should be suppressed for one hour . . . it would be treason"; and "Treason is a greater crime in republics than in monarchies. . . ."[7]

On February 21, Marshall delivered the opinion of a

unanimous court.⁸ The issue was limited: was the evidence offered adequate to warrant commitment on a charge of treason? Characteristically, Marshall proceeded to a broad definition of law. Beginning his definition, the chief justice turned to the Constitution. The words were restrictive; the intent had been to prevent "those calamities which result from the extension of treason to offences of minor importance." What acts constituted a levying of war? "War must actually have been levied against the United States. . . ." A conspiracy to levy war could not amount to treason, and the definition of such a crime was a legislative matter. The justice then entered this gloss:

> It is not the intention of the court to say that no individual can be guilty of this crime who has not appeared in arms against his country. On the contrary, if war be actually levied, that is, if a body of men be actually assembled for the purpose of effecting by force a treasonable purpose, all those who perform any part, however minute, or however remote from the scene of action, and who are actually leagued in the general conspiracy, are to be considered as traitors; but there must be an actual assemblage of men to constitute a levying of war.

Marshall would regret these words. The opinion was incomplete. Had the justice extended his opinion to include a statement of the correct method of proceeding against a person performing "any part, however minute, or however remote" from treasonable action, he would have saved himself the embarrassment of the charge that he reversed this opinion in the Burr trial.

The court then examined the evidence and found it insufficient to warrant commitment. Bollman and Swartout were free. Concluding, Marshall drove a barb at Jefferson:

> If those whose duty it is to protect the nation, by prosecuting offenders against the laws, shall suppose those who have been charged with treason to be proper objects of punishment, they

will, when possessed of less exceptionable testimony, and when able to say at what place the offence had been committed, institute fresh proceedings against them.

Official Washington, from the President down, had followed the proceedings with intense interest. Reactions were mixed. Jefferson vented spleen by censuring sharply a marine officer for entertaining Swartout after his release. Republican congressmen muttered threats of impeachment and discussed a constitutional amendment taking away all Supreme Court criminal jurisdiction. The administration was attacked in the House of Representatives. A resolution securing the writ of habeas corpus touched off a three-day debate. Sharp-tongued John Randolph lashed out with the accusation that Jefferson and the Republicans had abandoned the defense of civil liberties: "The people of this country after two or three juggles of this kind, will be apt to conclude that federalism or republicanism depends on being in or out of Government. . . ." He went on to pillory Wilkinson, a favorite target.[9]

These preliminaries guaranteed that the trial of Aaron Burr would be no deliberate and temperate inquiry into the law of treason.

Originally, Burr had been committed for a misdemeanor only. Let to bail, he was bound over to appear before the Richmond circuit court. The interval was not quiet. Before the trial, Marshall attended a dinner party and found Aaron Burr a fellow guest. Though a great impropriety, it is hardly evidence that Marshall had determined to release Burr in any event.[10] Jefferson himself planned the prosecution.[11] To support District Attorney George Hay, the government retained William Wirt and Alexander McRae. Burr, a competent lawyer himself, retained distinguished counsel: Edmund Randolph, John Wickham, Benjamin Botts, Charles Lee, and indefatigable Luther Martin. The argument at bar would be of a dual nature. Intermixed with an extensive and exhaustive analysis of the law would be frequent appeals to political prejudice. The argument would be interspersed with impassioned declamation addressed to the audience rather than to the bench. Over this tournament of wit, legal erudition, and oratory, John Marshall presided.

People flocked to the scene of the spectacle. "I had just ridden my first circuit as an incipient man of law, when, like a vast multitude of others, including the flower of the land, I hastened up to Richmond, to witness a scene of highest interest." [12] The business got off to a flying start and revealed the defense strategy of contesting every procedural point. Burr protested that the grand jury had been summoned irregularly. The court removed several jurors. This was countered by the district attorney with a motion to commit Burr for treason. A long, spirited debate developed on a motion to commit. The defense forced Hay to prove an overt act of levying war. Several witnesses to the assemblage on Blennerhassett's Island testified. Things moved slowly, and the prosecution became embarrassed by the absence of the star witness, General Wilkinson. The grand jury adjourned.[13] A reporter for a New York paper wrote ". . . you can little conceive the talents for procrastination that have been exhibited in this affair. . . . We are now enjoying a kind of suspension of hostilities. . . ." [14]

When the grand jury reassembled, the defense seized the initiative. They asked the court to subpoena the President in order to obtain papers they thought relevant. In argument, Luther Martin pounded Jefferson. He accused him of prejudging Burr. "He has let slip the dogs of war, the hell hounds of persecution to hunt down my friend." Wirt, no mean orator, responded by charging the court with permitting itself to be a forum for "perpetual phillipics against government." After more of this cross fire, Marshall issued the subpoena. With dignity, Jefferson refused to respond.[15]

After three weeks, Wilkinson arrived and was sent immediately to the grand jury. While the jury sat, counsel wrangled over a defense motion to attach Wilkinson for intimidating witnesses and rifling a post office to obtain evidence. Wilkinson's reputation was so bad that John Randolph, the jury foreman, almost convinced the jurors to return a presentment against the general. On June 24, the jury returned four true bills indicting Burr and Blennerhassett for treason and misdemeanor.[16]

Thousands of words have been spilled over the questions of law and fact raised at this trial. The fundamental fact was that the indictment of Burr was faulty. The overt act alleged was the assembly on Blennerhassett's Island. Burr was indicted as having been present. He had not been. From the beginning, the government built its case on a false basis. They had, in effect, to argue that he was constructively present, a doctrine unknown to the common law. Had the jury ultimately returned a verdict of guilty, the judgment undoubtedly would have been arrested.

Two weeks were consumed in seating a jury. Of the first venire of thirty-six, only four were selected. A second venire was being rapidly exhausted when Burr accepted several who had expressed opinions of his guilt.[17]

Hay, opening for the government,[18] said the real question was, what constituted a levying of war? Building on the Bollman-Swartout opinion, he argued that the act of assembling for the purpose of effecting by force a treasonable design amounted to levying war. Arms and the use of force were not necessary ingredients. All persons engaged were traitors. These, he said, were settled maxims of the common law, reinforced by the recent decision of the Supreme Court. The attorney unfolded the government's case: he would first prove a treasonable design, then that there had been an assembly to carry out that design, and then that Burr had been the mastermind. Over defense counsel objection, Hay began to call his witnesses.

Hay first attempted to prove the intent. His first witnesses were prominent men whom Burr had sought out because of their known discontent with the administration. He called "General" William Eaton. The "general" stated flatly that Burr had approached him with a proposition to revolutionize the trans-Appalachian west. Eaton also told of his fantastic effort to head off the revolt by suggesting to Jefferson that Burr be given a major diplomatic post.[19] Commodore Truxton, who was to have been Burr's admiral, knew nothing of the treason. Burr had tried to convince him of the legality of a private filibustering raid in the event of war with Spain. Truxton was never drawn in.[20]

Peter Taylor, Blennerhassett's gardener, told a long story. The gist was this: the principals, Burr and Blennerhassett, had been absent from the island when the Ohio militia began to move. Taylor had borne a letter from Mrs. Blennerhassett to her husband. This mission took him to Cincinnati and Lexington, where he located the men. His testimony created a vague sense of conspiracy and was more material to the government's case against Blennerhassett. Apparently the rank and file of those enlisted thought they were bound for the Washita lands. The other object, or objects, were to be revealed after the expedition was in motion. Burr was to be King of Mexico. Blennerhassett, a comic-opera conspirator, once spoke of a letter as containing "high treason." [21]

Colonel George Morgan and two of his sons testified next. Burr had made a bid to enlist this powerful west-Pennsylvania family. To them he had spoken generally of military affairs and the inevitability of western separation.[22] Five other witnesses testified about the assembly on the island. Their testimony proved that the men were armed, that they thought themselves bound for the Washita or Mexico, that they were prepared to resist the Ohio militia, and that Aaron Burr had not been on the island for at least six weeks prior to the action described.[23]

Government counsel then moved to introduce collateral evidence to prove Burr's responsibility for the treasonable assembly. Here the fundamental weakness of the prosecution was revealed. They were striving for a conviction under an indictment that charged Burr with an overt act by introducing evidence showing his responsibility only and, in fact, specifically denying his participation in the overt act. Burr's counsel moved to arrest the evidence. This sparked a ten-day debate that ended with Marshall's second opinion on the law of treason.

To make a précis of the briefs of defense and prosecution is no mean task. The argument was exhaustive, sometimes brilliant, but often redundant. Both sides willingly departed from the business at hand to loose a political blast. Counsel coursed through the books like a pack of fine hounds, leaving no trail nor hint of scent unexplored. They bequeathed eight hundred pages as trophy of the chase. The major questions at issue were these: what acts constituted the crime of levying war; were persons engaged in a treasonable conspiracy, though not present at the act alleged in the indictment, culpable; to what extent was the common law applicable in America?

The extent to which the common law was applicable in federal courts was then a vexed question. Defense argued that there was no general federal common law; that treason against the United States was a newly created offense and should be defined without reference to the common law.[24] Government counsel conceded that there could be no common law crime. They contended, though, that since the authors of the Constitution had cast their definition in the words of a statute that clarified the common law, it was proper to go to that law for the meaning of terms.[25] In spite of this conflict of opinion, both sides went to common law to prove their points.

Addressing themselves to the question, what constituted

a levying of war, counsel went to the same books and obtained different answers. The defense definition insisted on these elements: an actual assemblage embodied with treasonable intent; the presence of the paraphernalia of war, though small arms in the frontier community were not necessarily military weapons; a real application of force.[26] The government contended that arms and the application of force were not necessary ingredients of the crime of levying war if the treasonable intent of the men assembled could be proved.[27]

The conflict of law put to the bench on the question of the elements of levying war, technical as it was, was clear and simple compared with the arguments advanced when counsel addressed themselves to the problem of the guilt of an aider, abettor, or procurer of treason.

The prosecution made a strong case. Turning to English law they found in all of the elementary writers from Coke to Blackstone the maxim "in treason all are principals." They drove the point home by citing the part of the Bollman and Swartout decision stating that once war was levied, all who participated in the conspiracy must share the guilt.[28] Hard pressed, defense counsel rejected the American opinion as *obiter dictum*. With ingenuity, they traced the English doctrine relative to accessories to its presumed sources. They attempted to force the prosecution to stand on bad precedent.[29] Further, they cited the Judiciary Act of 1789. Here Congress had distinguished between accessory and principal in lesser crimes. Should not the same logic apply to the great crime? [30]

In the context of argument over accessory and principal, defense counsel made their strong procedural points. They contended that the indictment needed to be specific; that it had to charge the accused with an act that he had actually committed; that it had to be laid in the county where the offense occurred.[31] Both reason and justice, they urged, would exclude the indictment of an accessory as a principal or the indictment of an accessory before the principal was tried. The prosecution answered these points lamely, arguing a constructive presence.[32]

Toward the end of the thirteenth week of the proceedings, Luther Martin ended the argument, and Marshall delivered the opinion of the court. The opinion is much misunderstood. Three now venerable myths must fall before any objective inquiry: that Marshall was ignorant of common law; that he cut off the possibility of application of the common law constructive treasons in the federal jurisdiction; that in a labored, tortured opinion, he alone saved Aaron Burr from the noose.

If knowledge of the common law is proved by sheer quantity of citation, Marshall was ignorant. He believed, as did his most learned contemporaries, that precedents were not common law;[33] that law consisted of a substratum of principles illuminated by precedent. In the argument he had heard, precedent had befogged rather than clarified principle. Marshall thought it perfectly proper to go to the common law for the meaning of the term "levying war." Unaided, the judge, seeking illumination of the principles of the law of treason in the adjudged cases, faced an overwhelming task; thousands of pages of the *State Trials* stood as a monument of a centuries long, erratic effort to shield the sovereign. But there was no need to plunge without a guide into that wilderness. The trail had been blazed by "those celebrated elementary writers, who have stated the principles of the law."[34] Marshall's opinion is a masterful, critical analysis of those elementary writers.

What, then, was the meaning of the words, "Treason against the United States shall consist only in levying war against them"? The term "levying war" could be defined without reference to legal authority. "War is an appeal from reason to the sword; and he who makes the appeal evidences the fact by the use of the means." Marshall then put the common-sense definition to the test of case and commentary. Coke, Hale, Hawkins, Foster, and Blackstone concurred. "It must be a warlike assemblage, carrying the appearance of force, and in a situation to practice hostility." The American judges, Iredell, Paterson, Peters, and Chase, "required the actual exercise of force." Had the Supreme Court arrested this stream of precedent in the case of Bollman and Swartout? Marshall thought not and drew from the opinion those statements that went to the point: "To constitute the crime, war must be actually levied." Force, then, was a necessary ingredient of levying war.[35]

The further question necessarily came, was the aider, abettor, accessory, or procurer of a treasonable assemblage in fact a traitor? Crucial to the question were the words from the Bollman and Swartout case:

It is not the intention of the court to say that no individual can be guilty of this crime who had not appeared in arms against his country. On the contrary, if war be actually levied, that is, if a body of men be actually assembled for the purpose of effecting by force a treasonable object, all those who perform any part, however minute, or however remote from the scene of action, and who are actually leagued in the general conspiracy, are to be considered as traitors.

On the one hand, Marshall had been encouraged to dismiss this as mere *obiter dictum;* on the other, to regard it as having brought in the English doctrine that in treason all are principals. He declined both invitations. This is the least forceful part of the opinion. Obviously, under English law an accessory before or after the fact was a traitor. But this was not American law. Whether a procurer or other accessory to a treason might be a traitor, the justice said, was an interesting question. Whether procurement was a "minute" part of levying war was a question for the Supreme Court to decide when it was hearing a case in point. Marshall contended, with technical propriety, that a ruling on the point was not essential to the motion before the court.[36]

This was the sum of Marshall's ruling on the substantive nature of treason. It has become a commonplace to say that he arrested the growth of the common law doctrine of constructive treason. This is not true. A constructive treason is one based on judicial extension of 25 Edward III. Actually, there was no issue of constructive treason in the Burr case. In his review of the law, Marshall analyzed the American cases that had brought in the doctrine of a constructive levying of war, without objection.[37] The one constructive treason that could apply in America, the doctrine that raised a riot to oppose the execution of a general law to treason, remained good law—as it has to this day.

The outcome of the Burr trial did not depend on a definition of the substantive law. The issue was resolved on an important procedural point. Burr stood indicted as having been present at Blennerhassett's Island. In fact he had not been. The prosecution had argued that a general charge of levying war was adequate and that Burr had been, in effect, constructively present. The defense insisted that the charge needed to be specific and proved as laid.

Marshall made three points relative to the timing and form of indictment: that the conviction of the principal must precede the indictment of the accessory; that the indictment must be specific; that the charge must be proved as laid.

Whatever the doctrine of English law relative to accessory and principal, the indictment of the latter must come first.[38] The indictment must charge specifically time, place, and presence. Here, Marshall moved with authority through the commentators. He rejected as inapplicable the dictum of Hale that a person absent from an event could be indicted as present if he had caused the action. The chief justice found such a proposition unsupported by adjudicated cases and restricted its application to treason by counterfeiting, a matter irrelevant in the Burr case.[39] The prosecution had argued by analogy from certain felonies that the accused did not actually have to be present. Marshall went to the books and concluded that in such cases the accused would have to be in a position to render actual assistance as the crime was being perpetrated. The chief justice nailed down his points with reference to the American Constitution and statutes. The trial should be "in the state and district wherein the crime shall have been committed." The eighth amendment required that the accused be "informed of the nature and cause of the accusation." [40] Marshall granted the motion to arrest the evidence.

However one approaches the issue, he must conclude that the indictment of Aaron Burr was faulty. Certainly the barrier that Marshall here erected to general indictments and constructive presence was consistent with reason and justice. In this light, the charge that "Marshall . . . stepped between Burr and death" [41] and by so doing created "the one serious blemish on his judicial career," [42] is erroneous.

The jury returned a special verdict: ". . . Aaron Burr is not proved to be guilty under this indictment by any evidence submitted to us. We therefore find him not guilty." Burr objected, and it was entered on the record "not guilty." This result was ill-received. Jefferson put the matter before Congress in a special message. He asked the legislature to determine "whether the defect was in the testimony, in the law, or in the administration of the law." [43] In the Senate, Edward Tiffin introduced a constitutional amendment fixing the tenure of judges for a term of years and making them removable by a two-thirds vote of both houses.[44] A special committee investigated the conduct of John Smith, an accomplice of Burr, and the Senate moved his expulsion.[45] William Giles introduced a bill in the Senate defining the law of treason. In debate he assaulted Marshall. The justice strove to establish judicial supremacy, but acted like a "miserable political intriguer, scrambling for power." [46] This was the last Republican thrust in Jefferson's campaign to emasculate the judiciary.

The decision in the Burr case made no change in the procedural law. The opinion had insisted on the proof of a specific overt act by two witnesses. At Marshall's hand, the treason law remained what it had been.

8

Lese Majesty in the American Republic

During the first century of American colonization, English judges sharpened the main, available weapon for the protection of the sovereign—the law of treason. At their hands, constructive treason hardened into fixed rules. Crown lawyers regularly used the treason law to repress political opposition.

From their inception, the American provincial governments experienced resistance. In the earliest days, legislators protected their infant jurisdictions with codes that bore little resemblance to the parent law. These early codes did not endure and hence had little or no long-range effect on the development of American law. As the colonies matured, the assemblies tended increasingly to pattern their laws of treason, in both substantive and procedural aspects, after English models. The Colonial magistrates used the common law whenever circumstances demanded a dramatic repression of opposition. By the eve of the American Revolution, the English law of treason had been transferred substantially to the trans-Atlantic dominions. No "frontier" hypothesis can explain the development of the Colonial law under this head.

After 1763, British efforts to force the Colonies into a renovated commercial empire touched off resistance that led to revolution. In one area, at least, George III and his ministers inflexibly pursued a consistent policy. At all times they regarded the resistance as criminal and urged their agents to create an intimidating example by trying American leaders as traitors. When this failed, Lord North used treason to justify the punitive statutes that brought on the Revolution. Long before independence was declared, Washington saw that the American war effort would be feeble unless sovereign powers were assumed. Under the general's direction, the army punished military traitors and exposed civilian disloyalists. Pushed by the army, Congress demanded allegiance and defined treason. In so doing, it *de facto* declared independence. Lacking civilian courts, the Congress asked the states to define treason and to punish breaches of allegiance.

Following the congressional suggestion, the states defined treason by statute. The tendency of the laws was to limit treason to two heads of the common law: adhering to the enemy, giving him aid and comfort; and levying war against the state. Many of the legislatures, in attempting to define adherence, described virtually every act of assistance as treason. In addition to the treason statutes, the states passed laws defining as less than treasonable a long series of acts of resistance and opposition to government. If these latter statutes are regarded as sufficiently of the genus treason to be included as species, then the treason law of the revolutionary period exceeded the common law in its severity on the substantive side. If, however, these statutes are seen as attempts to establish, in time of great emergency, a series of acts as less than treason, then they may be regarded as limitations of the common law of treason. Most authors dealing with the subject have preferred the former view. I prefer the latter, though the evidence either way is scanty and in no way conclusive.

There was, though, one substantial difference between the treason statutes and the other laws punishing disloyal acts. The penalty for treason was death. Though a few of the statutes establishing the lesser crimes described them as felonies punishable by death, the majority of the laws prescribed lesser punishments such as fine and imprisonment. Certainly the difference between life and death was substantial. On the procedural side, the states brought in the English statute of 1696 and made innovations to further secure the rights of individuals.

A close scrutiny of the application of the treason law by state executive and legislative officials indicates that extreme Toryism was a condition created by military action. Movements of the armies determined the loyalty of whole sections. A sudden surge by the British would convert a region, even most of a state, to Toryism. A solid American counterattack would reverse the trend.

Study of the treason law in action leads to a revision of the notion that state officials rode roughshod over procedural rights and conducted a reign of terror. The evidence establishes a record of judicial moderation. In applying the law of treason reluctantly, state officials established a pervasive precedent: political opposition, even of a disloyal nature, was not to be avenged by blood.

In establishing the substantive and procedural law of treason for a new nation, the Constitution-makers turned to the ancient statute of Edward III. Though it is commonly assumed that their intent was to restrict the law, the evidence is equivocal. The paramount unanswered question was, what part of English case law would apply in the new jurisdiction? Federalist judges answered the question by accepting that part of the common law that expanded the definition of levying war to include aggravated riots against government. It was on the side of evidence that the Constitution-makers and judges restricted government.

Through the 1790's, policy, rather than strict law, set the important precedents. The great state trials of the early years of the Republic were closely related to the politics of the time, and those politics were violently partisan. The risings against Federalist laws wrote two basic precedents large upon the wall: political rather than direct action was the agency for changing government; political opposition, even of a criminal nature, was not to be chastised at the gallows. Had the law of treason been regularly applied during the years of the Republican-Federalist conflict, American political parties would probably have become mere factions using "their alternate malignity on each other." Instead, the nation preferred Jefferson's advice, refusing to countenance political intolerance capable of engendering bitter and bloody persecution.

Notes

CHAPTER 1

1. *The Federalist No. 43* in E. H. Scott (ed.), *The Federalist and Other Constitutional Papers by Hamilton, Jay, Madison and other Statesmen of Their Time; with a full Index* (2 vols.; Chicago: Albert, Scott and Co., 1894), I, 240; Baron de Montesquieu, *The Spirit of Laws* (Worcester, Mass.: Isaiah Thomas, Jr., 1802), I, 223.

2. 25 Edward III st. 5, c. 2.

3. William S. Holdsworth, *A History of English Law* (London: Methuen and Co., Ltd., 1931), VIII, 309–21.

4. King v. John Twyn (1663). Complete bibliographical information for all cases cited is contained in the Table of Cases.

5. Algernon Sydney's Case (1683).

6. King v. Peter Messenger, *et al.* (1668).

7. 7 & 8 William III, c. 3.

8. George N. Clark, *The Later Stuarts, 1660–1714* (Oxford: The Clarendon Press, 1934), p. 3.

9. Thomas B. Howell (ed.), *A Complete Collection of State Trials and Proceedings for High Treason and Other Crimes and Misdemeanors from the Earliest Period to the Present Time* (London: Longman, Hurst, Rees, Orme, Brown and Green, 1809–28), XV, 1, hereafter cited as Howell, *State Trials*.

10. Queen v. Francis Willis; Queen v. George Purchase (1710), Queen v. Dammaree *et al.* Perhaps the clearest statement of the doctrine of constructive war was made in the charge to the jury in Dammaree's case.

11. 1 George I, c. 5.

12. Case of Lord George Gordon (1781); see especially Mansfield's charge.

13. 36 George III, c. 7.

14. King v. William Anderton (1693); King v. Lord Preston (1691). These constructive treasons remained good law through the eighteenth century; see King v. Thomas Hardy (1794). It

should be noted that in this case, as in Gordon's case, the jury returned a verdict of innocent, reflecting, perhaps, a dislike of the law as stated by the judges. See also the Case of Henry and John Sheares. There had been considerable confusion relative to the doctrine of treasonable words. After the Revolution of 1688, distinctions were made between spoken and written words (Holdsworth, *A History of English Law* [London: Methuen Co., Ltd., 1931], VIII, 316–17). Eighteenth-century commentators did not agree (William Blackstone, *Commentaries on the Laws of England* [Oxford: The Clarendon Press, 1778], IV, 79–81, hereafter cited as *Commentaries;* cf. Michael Foster, *A Report of Some Proceedings on the Commission for the Trial of the Rebels in the year 1746, in the county of Surry; and of other Crown Cases: to which is added Discourses upon a few Branches of the Crown Law* [London: Printed for E. and R. Brookes, 1792], p. 200, hereafter cited as *Crown Law*). On the whole, the crown preferred to attack verbal resistance with the law of seditious libel (Howell, *State Trials,* XIX–XXII, *passim*).

15. Willard Hurst, "Treason in the United States," *Harvard Law Review,* LVIII (1944), 226–72; Nathaniel Bouton (ed.), *Documents and Records Relating to the Province of New Hampshire, 1623–1800* (Concord, N.H.; Published by authority of the legislature, 1867–73), I, 383; J. Hammond Trumbull and Charles J. Hoadly (eds.), *The Public Records of the Colony of Connecticut* (Hartford, Conn.: Lockwood and Brainard Co., 1850–90), I, 78; Charles J. Hoadly (ed.), *Records of the Colony or Jurisdiction of New Haven* (Hartford, Conn.: Lockwood and Co., 1858), II, 577–78.

16. Hurst, "Treason in the United States," *Harvard Law Review,* LVIII (1944), 226–72; for example, William L. Saunders (ed.), *Colonial Records of North Carolina (1662–1776)* (Raleigh, N.C.: P. M. Hale, 1886–90), XXIII, 319–22; *The Acts and Resolves, Public and Private of the Province of Massachusetts Bay: to which are Prefixed the Charters of the Province* (Boston: Wright and Potter, 1869–1922), I, 55, 255; Robert C. Cumming (ed.), *The Colonial Laws of New York from the Year 1664 to the Revolution* (Albany, N.Y.: J. B. Lyon, 1894), I, 575; *Laws of the State of Delaware from the Fourteenth Day of October, One Thousand Seven Hundred, to the Eighteenth Day of August, One Thousand Seven Hundred and Ninety-Seven* (New Castle, Del.: Samuel and John Adams, 1816), I, 64; James T. Mitchell and Henry Flanders (eds.), *The Statutes at Large of Pennsylvania from*

Notes

1682 to 1801 (Harrisburg, Penn.: C. M. Busch, 1896–19——), III, 199; Thomas Cooper (ed.), *The Statutes at Large of South Carolina* (Columbia, S.C.: A. S. Johnston, 1836–41), II, 714, 747; *Acts and Laws of His Majesties Colony of Connecticut in New England* (Hartford, Conn.: Reissued by Case, Lockwood and Brainard Co., 1901), pp. 13–14.

17. Hurst, "Treason in the United States," *Harvard Law Review*, LVIII (1944), 226–72; for example, Saunders, *Colonial Records of North Carolina*, XXIII, 319–22; *The Acts and Resolves of Massachusetts Bay*, I, 55, 255; Cumming, *Colonial Laws of New York*, III, 1050, 1077, 1121; Julius Goebel and T. Raymond Naughton, *Law Enforcement in Colonial New York, a Study in Criminal Procedure, 1664–1776* (New York: Commonwealth Fund, 1944), pp. 85, 241–44.

18. Cumming, *Colonial Laws of New York*, I, 223–24; William Hening (ed.), *The Statutes at Large, Being a Collection of all the Laws of Virginia from the First Session of the Legislature in the Year 1619* (Richmond, Va., New York, and Philadelphia: Samuel Pleasant, Franklin Press, J. and B. Cochran, George Cochran, Thomas Desilver, 1809–23), III, 10–12, hereafter cited as *The Statutes of Virginia*.

19. By court-martial, King v. Thomas Young and eleven others (Va., 1676–77); by civil trial, King v. Giles Bland and eight others (Va., 1676–77). Though there has been great difference of opinion ever since the event concerning Berkeley's policy, particularly in regard to method, the English commissioners were in perfect accord that there had been a treasonable levying of war. John W. Fortescue and W. Noel Sainsbury (eds.), *Calendar of State Papers, Colonial Series, America and West Indies, 1677–1680* (London: Longman and Co., 1860–19——), pp. 37, 42.

20. King v. Benjamin Merrill *et al.* (N.C., 1771). Though in the *Virginia Gazette,* Nov. 6, 1771, it is stated that the indictments came under a provincial statute modifying the local riot act.

21. King v. Jacob Leisler (N.Y., 1691); King v. Jacob Milborne (N.Y., 1691); but some of his adherents were tried for riot, implying constructed war.

22. King v. John Binckson ("Long Finn") (N.Y., 1669).

23. King v. Sommersett Davies *et al.* (Va., 1683).

24. King v. William Prendergast (N.Y., 1765); King v. Elisha Cole (N.Y., 1767).

25. King v. Nicholas Bayard (N.Y., 1702).

26. King v. Francis Rumbouts (N.Y., 1682).

27. King v. William Dyer (N.Y., 1682).

28. King v. Sommersett Davies *et al.* (Va., 1685); King v. Francis Rumbouts (N.Y., 1682); King v. Elisha Cole (N.Y., 1767); King v. William Dyer (N.Y., 1682), transfer of the case from the Mayor's Court on ground of inadequate jurisdiction.

29. King v. Benjamin Merrill (N.C., 1771); King v. William Prendergast (N.Y., 1765); King v. Jacob Leisler (N.Y., 1691); King v. Nicholas Bayard (N.Y., 1702); King v. Giles Bland and eight others (Va., 1676–77); using the special commission, the government could name the time and place where specified commissioners would sit.

30. King v. Nicholas Bayard (N.Y., 1702); the outline in King v. William Prendergast (N.Y., 1765); King v. John Gunter and nine others (Va., 1663).

31. King v. Jacob Leisler (N.Y., 1691). At English law, if a person stood mute to his indictment he could be subjected to the torture of the *peine;* successive weights were added to his body until he made a plea or died.

32. At least three colonies re-enacted its provisions. Mitchell and Flanders, *Statutes at Large of Pennsylvania,* III, 200; Cooper, *Statutes at Large of South Carolina,* II, 539, 717, 747; Saunders, *Colonial Records of North Carolina,* XXIII, 319–25; In re Beverly (Va., 1682); King v. Nicholas Bayard (N.Y., 1702).

33. King v. Nicholas Bayard (N.Y., 1702); King v. William Prendergast (N.Y., 1765); *The Perpetual Laws of the Commonwealth of Massachusetts, from the Establishment of its Constitution to the First Session of the General Court in A.D. 1788* (Worcester, Mass.: Isaiah Thomas, 1788), p. 263.

34. King v. Nicholas Bayard (N.Y., 1702); King v. Sommersett Davies *et al.* (Va., 1683); Tryon recommended that Benjamin Merrill's heirs have his estate; King v. Jacob Leisler (N.Y., 1691); King v. Richard Lawrence (Va., 1685); King v. Jacob Milborne (N.Y., 1691).

35. King v. Jacob Milborne (N.Y., 1691); King v. Benjamin Merrill *et al.* (N.C., 1771); King v. William Prendergast (N.Y., 1765); King v. Jacob Leisler (N.Y., 1691).

36. Tryon reprieved six condemned Regulators during the king's pleasure. In the cases of Leisler and Milborne, a petition to Privy Council was referred to the Lords of Trade where permission was granted to apply to Parliament for reversal of attainder. Privy Council removed the sentence of Nicholas Bayard.

37. For example, James Emmot in King v. Nicholas Bayard

argued that the evidence did not meet the requirements of the Statute of 1696 and that 1 Henry IV c. 10 limits treason to the categories established by 25 Edward III c. 2, further that the king's counsel may not challenge jurors without cause, whereupon the solicitor general cited King v. Peter Cook. Benjamin Kissam, summing up for the crown in King v. William Prendergast cited Foster, Keiling, and Hawkins. See also the opinion of the attorney general relative to the degree of criminality of the Regulators (Saunders, *Colonial Records of North Carolina*, VIII, 251–53). The revolutionary cases also give evidence of extensive familiarity with English precedent. See Pennsylvania v. Abraham Carlisle where James Wilson cites Foster and Hale, *Law of Nisi Prius*, Vaughan's case. The attorney general draws heavily on Foster. Blackstone and Eden are cited, as are statutes from Edward I to Anne.

CHAPTER 2

1. Minutes of the Governor and Council of New York, XXVI, 16, in New York State Library, Albany; Clarence E. Carter (ed.), *The Correspondence of General Thomas Gage with the Secretaries of State, 1763–1775* (New Haven, Conn.: Yale University Press, 1931), I, 68.
2. New York *Post-Boy*, Nov. 7, 1764; Jan. 9, 1766; Edmund B. O'Callaghan and John R. Brodhead (eds.), *Documents Relative to the Colonial History of the State of New York* (Albany, N.Y.: Weed, Parsons and Co., 1853–87), VII, 771–72; Wilbur C. Abbott, *New York in the American Revolution* (New York: Charles Scribner's Sons, 1929), 53–58.
3. Minutes of the Governor and Council of New York, XXVI, 39–42.
4. *Ibid.*, pp. 18–19, 44–45.
5. O'Callaghan and Brodhead, *Documents . . . Colonial History of . . . New York*, VII, 773–74, 810–12; G. D. Scull (ed.), *The Montresor Journals* (New York: New York Historical Society, 1881), pp. 339, 382; Carter, *Gage Correspondence*, I, 71–73, 78–79, 81–82.
6. Carter, *Gage Correspondence*, I, 78–79.
7. King v. William Prendergast (N.Y., 1765).
8. William Cobbett (ed.), *Parliamentary History of England, from the Norman Conquest, in 1066 to the year 1803* (London: Longman's and Co., 1806–20), XVI, 161, hereafter cited as *Han-*

123

sard (from the name of the official printer of parliamentary proceedings).

9. *Ibid.*, p. 170.

10. *Ibid.*, p. 172.

11. *Bowdoin and Temple Papers* (Collections of the Massachusetts Historical Society), Ser. 6, IX, 83.

12. George Bancroft, *History of the United States from the Discovery of the American Continent* (Boston: Little, Brown, 1834–75), VI, 148.

13. William S. Taylor and John H. Pringle (eds.), *Correspondence of William Pitt* (London: John Murray, 1839–40), III, 187.

14. These events are described in Edward Channing, *A History of the United States* (New York: Macmillan Co., 1905–25), III, 81–113.

15. Harry A. Cushing (ed.), *The Writings of Samuel Adams* (New York: G. P. Putnam's Sons, 1904–8), I, 184–88.

16. Alden Bradford (ed.), *Speeches of the Governors of Massachusetts, from 1765 to 1775; and the Answers of the House of Representatives to the Same* (Boston: Russell and Gardiner, 1818), p. 150.

17. *The Annual Register, a Review of Public Events at Home and Abroad* (London: J. Dodsley, 1758–19——), p. 235 (events of 1768).

18. Thomas Hutchinson, *The History of Massachusetts Bay* (London: John Murray, 1828), III, 205–12; *Papers Relating to Public Events in Massachusetts Preceding the American Revolution* (Philadelphia: Printed for The Seventy-Six Society, 1856), 101–5.

19. *Ibid.*, pp. 56–57, 63–66, 94–95, 101–5.

20. Bancroft, *History of the United States*, VI, 178.

21. 35 Henry VIII, c. 2.

22. Edward Channing (ed.), *The Barrington-Bernard Correspondence and Illustrative Matter 1760–1770 Drawn from the Papers of Sir Francis Bernard (Sometime Governor of Massachusetts-Bay)* (Cambridge, Mass.: Harvard University Press, 1912), p. 166.

23. Bancroft, *History of the United States*, VI, 230, 233–34; Channing, *History of the United States*, III, 98–99. A search in the Public Record Office has failed to uncover Hillsborough's letter or the answer of the law officers (Robert Stevens to author, May 8, 1951). Citations to original documents in the Public Rec-

ord Office are based on notes taken by Robert Stevens of London, England.

24. *Hansard,* XVI, 466–70.

25. *Ibid.,* pp. 476–79.

26. *Ibid.,* pp. 479–80.

27. *Ibid.,* pp. 446–92.

28. *Ibid.,* p. 492.

29. *Ibid.,* p. 494.

30. William J. Smith (ed.), *The Grenville Papers: being the Correspondence of Richard Grenville Earl Temple K. G., and the Right Hon. George Grenville, their Friends and Contemporaries* (London: n.p., 1852–53), IV, 391.

31. Carter, *Gage Correspondence,* II, 509–10.

32. Bancroft, *History of the United States,* VI, 251.

33. Channing, *Barrington-Bernard Correspondence,* p. 184.

34. *Ibid.,* p. 197.

35. Kate M. Rowland, *The Life of George Mason, 1725–1792* (New York: G. P. Putnam's Sons, 1892), I, 137.

36. Channing, *Barrington-Bernard Correspondence,* p. 291.

37. *Bowdoin and Temple Papers,* pp. 132–33.

38. John R. Bartlett (ed.), *Records of the Colony of Rhode Island and Providence Plantations in New England* (Providence, R.I.: A. C. Greene and Brothers, 1856–65), VII, 191–92.

39. Historical Manuscripts Commission (HMC), Great Britain, *Fourteenth Report,* Appendix, Part 10, p. 185.

40. Correspondence of the secretary of state for the colonies with the attorney and solicitor general, 1772–81, PRO CO 5/159, 22, Public Record Office, London.

41. *Ibid.,* pp. 26–27.

42. HMC, *Fourteenth Report,* Appendix, Part 10, p. 88.

43. *Acts of the Privy Council of England, Colonial Series* (Hereford: Great Britain, 1908–12), V, 365–67.

44. Proprieties, PRO CO 5/1278, 227–37.

45. HMC, *Fourteenth Report,* Appendix, Part 10, p. 91.

46. Bartlett, *Records of the Colony of Rhode Island,* VII, 103–4.

47. The commissioners' report is in *ibid.,* pp. 120 ff.

48. William R. Staples (ed.), *The Documentary History of the Destruction of the Gaspee* (Providence, R.I.: Knowles, Vose and Anthony, 1845), p. 55.

49. HMC, *Fourteenth Report,* Appendix, Part 10, p. 195; PRO CO 5/169, 16 (Library of Congress transcript).

50. *Ibid.,* p. 55.
51. *Acts of the Privy Council of England, Colonial Series,* V, 391–92.
52. HMC, *Report on Manuscripts in Various Collections,* VI, 269–70.
53. Peter O. Hutchinson (ed.), *The Diary and Letters of His Excellency Thomas Hutchinson* (London: S. Low, Marston, Searle, and Rivington, 1883–86), I, 183.
54. *Ibid.,* p. 219.
55. *Ibid.,* p. 245; Carter, *Gage Correspondence,* II, 160–61; HMC, *Report on the Marquis of Lothian,* pp. 290–91.
56. Carter, *Gage Correspondence,* II, 171–72; HMC, *Fourteenth Report,* Appendix, Part 10, p. 220; Hutchinson, *Diary,* I, 205, 207.
57. *Hansard,* XVIII, pp. 289, 292.
58. Samuel Johnson, *Taxation No Tyranny* (London: Printed for W. Strahan and T. Cadell, 1776).
59. Carter, *Gage Correspondence,* II, 160–61.
60. *Ibid.,* I, 359; II, 649.
61. *Ibid.,* I, 171–72.
62. HMC, *Eleventh Report,* Appendix, Part 5, p. 371.
63. PRO CO 5/159, 63 (Library of Congress transcript).
64. John R. Alden, *General Gage in America, Being Principally a History of His Role in the American Revolution* (Baton Rouge, La.: Louisiana State University Press, 1948), pp. 233–44.
65. Carter, *Gage Correspondence,* II, 181–83.
66. Alden, *General Gage in America,* pp. 242–43.
67. Carter, *Gage Correspondence,* I, 402.
68. HMC, *Eleventh Report,* Appendix, Part 5, p. 371.
69. PRO CO 5/159, 65–66, 72–73 (Library of Congress transcript).
70. HMC, *Fourteenth Report,* Appendix, Part 10, pp. 260, 283.
71. Carter, *Gage Correspondence,* II, 191–92. By this time the ministry had yet another opinion from Thurlow and Wedderburn (Feb. 2, 1775), reciting the acts of the Massachusetts Provincial Congress to be treason (PRO CO 5/159, 63 [Library of Congress transcript]).
72. Peter Force (ed.), *American Archives: Consisting of a collection of authentick records, state papers, debates, and letters* (Washington, D.C.: M. St. Claire and Peter Force), Ser. 4 (1837–46), II, 968–69, hereafter cited as Force, *American Archives.*

73. 14 George III, c. 19.
74. 14 George III, c. 45.
75. *Hansard,* XVII, 1200–1. The issue of treason at Boston appeared frequently in the debates on the Coercive Acts. *Ibid.,* pp. 1180, 1183, 1188, 1300–1, 1302.
76. Hutchinson, *Diary,* I, 265, 293, 297, 306.
77. *Ibid.,* p. 298.
78. *Hansard,* XVIII, 33.
79. *Ibid.,* p. 176.
80. *Ibid.,* pp. 222–24.
81. 15 George III, c. 10.
82. *Hansard,* XVIII, 299.
83. *Ibid.,* p. 300.
84. 15 George III, c. 18.
85. Force, *American Archives,* Ser. 4, III, 240–41. The part of the proclamation relative to traitorous correspondence was directed against men like "Junius Americanus" (Arthur Lee). HMC, *Fourteenth Report,* Appendix, Part 10, pp. 348, 349, 373, 379.
86. 16 George III, c. 5.
87. Quoted in Allen French, *The First Year of the American Revolution* (Boston: Houghton Mifflin Co., 1934), p. 424.
88. Ethan Allen, *A Narrative of Colonel Ethan Allen's Captivity, from the Time of His Being Taken by the British, near Montreal, on the 25th day of September, in the Year 1775, to the Time of his Exchange, on the 6th day of May, 1778* (Philadelphia: Printed for the author, 1799), p. 490.
89. At least none can be found. The order to attend is in PRO CO 5/159, 75.
90. Apparently Germain had made up his mind to release the men and merely asked the ministers to approve. HMC, *Report on the Manuscripts of Mrs. Stopford-Sackville* (London: Mackie and Co., 1904–10), I, 24.
91. Allen, *Narrative,* p. 495.
92. John C. Fitzpatrick (ed.), *The Writings of George Washington, from the original Manuscript Sources, 1745–1799* (Washington, D.C.: Government Printing Office, 1931–44), III, 416–17; hereafter cited as Fitzpatrick, *Writings of Washington.*
93. *Ibid.,* p. 418n.
94. *Ibid.,* pp. 430–31.
95. 17 George III, c. 9, extended by 18 George III, c. 1, and 19 George III, c. 1; *Hansard,* XIX, 3–51.
96. David D. Wallace, *The Life of Henry Laurens with a*

sketch of the Life of Lieutenant-Colonel John Laurens (New York: G. P. Putnam's Sons, 1915), pp. 362–89.

97. Benjamin F. Stevens (ed.), *Facsimiles of Manuscripts in European Archives Relating to America 1778–1783* (London: Malby and Sons, 1889–95), Nos. 920–22.

98. *Ibid.*, Nos. 986–90.

99. Henry Laurens, *A Narrative of the Capture of Henry Laurens, of his Confinement in the Tower of London &C. 1780, 1781, 1782* (Charleston, S.C.: S. G. Courtenay and Co., 1857–97), pp. 18–19.

CHAPTER 3

1. Worthington C. Ford and Gaillard Hunt (eds.), *Journals of the Continental Congress* (Washington, D.C.: Government Printing Office, 1904–28), II, 113, 116.

2. Fitzpatrick, *Writings of Washington,* III, 327, 331, 508n.

3. *Ibid.,* pp. 505–13.

4. Ford and Hunt, *Journals of the Continental Congress,* III, 265–67.

5. Allen French, *General Gage's Informers, New Material Upon Lexington & Concord. Benjamin Thompson as Loyalist & the Treachery of Benjamin Church, Jr.* (Ann Arbor, Mich.: University of Michigan Press, 1932), pp. 155–57.

6. Force, *American Archives,* Ser. 4, III, 1483.

7. Washington Papers (MS in the Library of Congress), Vol. XVIII, Oct. 2, 1775.

8. *Ibid.*

9. Fitzpatrick, *Writings of Washington,* IV, 9–11.

10. Force, *American Archives,* Ser. 4, III, 1479–86; Massachusetts Historical Society, *Warren-Adams Letters Being chiefly a correspondence among John Adams, Samuel Adams and James Warren* (Boston: Massachusetts Historical Society, 1917), LXXII, 180.

11. *Ibid.,* pp. 152–53.

12. Edmund C. Burnett (ed.), *Letters of Members of the Continental Congress* (Washington, D.C.: Carnegie Institute, 1921–36), I, 225; *Warren-Adams Letters,* pp. 137–38.

13. Ford and Hunt, *Journals of the Continental Congress,* III, 297, 334.

14. French, *Gage's Informers,* pp. 197–201.

15. Minutes of the Conference, Washington Papers (MS in the Library of Congress), Oct. 22, 1775; Force, *American Archives,* Ser. 4, III, 1158.

16. Ford and Hunt, *Journals of the Continental Congress,* III, 331.

17. Frank Moore (ed.), *Diary of the American Revolution, from Newspapers and Original Documents* (New York: Charles Scribner, 1860), I, 221.

18. *Ibid.,* p. 223.

19. *Ibid.*

20. *Ibid.,* I, 221, 223. See the case of the Negro, Jerry, in Charleston, South Carolina. An open Tory, he had publicly avowed his desire to join the king's troops. The state did not raise the issue of disloyalty, but tried him under a special criminal conspiracy statute on the charge of inciting a servile insurrection. HMC, *Fourteenth Report,* Appendix, Part 10, p. 354; Peter O. Hutchinson (ed.), *The Diary and Letters of His Excellency Thomas Hutchinson* (London: S. Low, Marston, Searle, and Rivington, 1883–86), I, 543.

21. The oath is printed in Samuel G. Arnold, *History of the State of Rhode Island and Providence Plantations* (New York: D. Appleton, 1859–60), II, 365.

22. Force, *American Archives,* Ser. 4, IV, 582–83.

23. Fitzpatrick, *Writings of Washington,* IV, 222.

24. Force, *American Archives,* Ser. 4, IV, 805–7.

25. *Ibid.,* V, 792; Burnett, *Letters of Members of The Continental Congress,* I, 389–90, 408; *Journals of the Provincial Congress, Provincial Committee of Safety and Council of Safety of the State of New York, 1777–1779* (Albany: T. Weed, 1886–88), I, 342–43, 379, hereafter cited as *Journals of . . . Provincial Congress . . . of New York;* Ford and Hunt, *Journals of the Continental Congress,* IV, 195.

26. Fitzpatrick, *Writings of Washington,* IV, 266, 293.

27. *Ibid.,* IV, 281.

28. Ford and Hunt, *Journals of the Continental Congress,* IV, 18–21.

29. Curtis P. Nettels, "A Link in the Chain of Events Leading to American Independence," *The William and Mary Quarterly,* Ser. 3, III (1946), 36–47.

30. Fitzpatrick, *Writings of Washington,* V, 182.

31. *Journals of . . . Provincial Congress . . . of New York,* I, 495–96.

32. Force, *American Archives,* Ser. 4, VI, 1158.
33. The connection between the Hickey plot and the treason resolves of June 24 is proved conclusively in Nettels, "Link in the Chain."
34. Ford and Hunt, *Journals of the Continental Congress,* V, 475–76.
35. *Journals of . . . Provincial Congress . . . of New York,* I, 517–19, 527, 530; II, 239.
36. See Nettels, "Link in the Chain."
37. Burnett, *Letters of Members of the Continental Congress,* I, 506.
38. *Pennsylvania Journal,* May 28, 1776; *Constitutional Gazette* (New York), June 19, 1776.
39. Hening, *Statutes of Virginia,* IX, 168.
40. *Laws of Maryland, Made Since M,DCC, LXIII, Consisting of Acts of Assembly under the Proprietary Government, Resolves of the Convention, the Declaration of Rights, the Constitution and Form of Government, the Articles of Confederation, And, Acts of the Assembly Since the Revolution* (Annapolis, Md.: Frederick Green, 1787), Feb. 1777, chap. 20 (n. p.), hereafter cited as *Laws of Maryland.* Benjamin P. Poore (ed.), *The Federal and State Constitutions, Colonial Charters and other Organic Laws of the United States* (Washington, D.C.: Government Printing Office, 1878), pp. 277, 1313, 1337–38.
41. See chapter 5.
42. For the statutes repeating or paraphrasing the statute of Edward III see: *Journals of . . . Provincial Congress . . . of New York,* I, 527; Mitchell and Flanders, *Statutes at Large of Pennsylvania,* IX, 18–20; *Perpetual Laws of Massachusetts,* pp. 357–62; *Laws of Maryland,* Feb. 1777, chap. 20; Henry H. Metcalf, *et al.* (eds.), *Laws of New Hampshire, Including Public and Private Acts and Resolves and the Royal Commission and Instructions, with Historical and Descriptive Notes, and an Appendix* (10 vols.; Manchester, Bristol, Concord: John B. Clarke *et al.,* 1904–22), IV, 128–30; Hening, *Statutes of Virginia,* IX, 168. For the statutes attempting more specific and detailed definitions, see: Mitchell and Flanders, *Statutes at Large of Pennsylvania,* IX, 45–47; James Iredell (ed.), *Laws of the State of North Carolina* (Edenton, N.C.: Hodge and Wills, 1799), pp. 284–86, hereafter cited as *Laws of North Carolina;* Charles J. Hoadly (ed.), *The Public Records of the State of Connecticut* (Hartford, Conn.: Lock-

wood and Co., 1858), I, 4; Peter Wilson (ed.), *Acts of the Council and General Assembly of the State of New Jersey from the Establishment of the Present Government, and Declaration of Independence to the End of the First Sitting of the Eighth Session on the 24th Day of December, 1783* (Trenton, N.J.: Isaac Collins, 1784), pp. 4–5, hereafter cited as *Acts of the New Jersey Council and General Assembly.*

43. Mitchell and Flanders, *Statutes at Large of Pennsylvania,* XI, 14–16.

44. Julian P. Boyd (ed.), *The Papers of Thomas Jefferson* (Princeton, N.J.: Princeton University Press, 1950–19——).

45. Iredell, *Laws of North Carolina,* pp. 284–86; Hoadly, *Public Records of the State of Connecticut,* I, 4; Mitchell and Flanders, *Statutes at Large of Pennsylvania,* IX, 45–47; Metcalf, *Laws of New Hampshire,* IV, 128–30; *Perpetual Laws of Massachusetts,* pp. 357–62.

46. Metcalf, *Laws of New Hampshire,* IV, 384–86.

47. Cf. Willard Hurst, "Treason in the United States," *Harvard Law Review,* LVIII (1944), 226–72, where Hurst regards these statutes as being so far of the genus treason as to be classified as extensions of the English law.

48. Hening, *Statutes of Virginia,* IX, 170.

49. *Laws of New York,* I, 370–71; Cooper, *Statutes at Large of South Carolina,* IV, 345.

50. *Laws of Maryland,* Feb. 1777, chap. 20; Hening, *Statutes of Virginia,* IX, 170; Metcalf, *Laws of New Hampshire,* IV, 75–76, 384–85. Wilson, *Acts of the New Jersey Council and General Assembly,* pp. 4–5; Iredell, *Laws of North Carolina,* pp. 284–86; Mitchell and Flanders, *Statutes at Large of Pennsylvania,* IX, 45–47.

51. See above, chapter 1.

52. For example, at the general quarter sessions in South Carolina and New Jersey (Cooper, *South Carolina Statutes at Large,* IV, 479); Wilson, *Acts of the Council and General Assembly of New Jersey,* pp. 43–52, 65–75, and this jurisdiction upheld 5 Cranch 185; by justice of the peace temporarily in North Carolina (Clark, *The State Records of North Carolina,* XXIV, 348–49).

53. Cooper, *Statutes at Large of South Carolina,* IV, 479; Hening, *Statutes of Virginia,* X, 387; *Laws of Maryland,* Feb. 1777, chap. 16; New York had used this commission in the colonial period. Melvil Dewey (ed.), *Calendar of Council Minutes, 1668–*

1783 (Albany, N.Y.: University of the State of New York, 1902), pp. 62, 163. The constitution of 1777 provided that the law of the colony was the law of the state.

54. Not necessarily judges, but persons "learned in the law."

55. For the English law, see: Edward Coke, *The Third Part of the Institutes of the Laws of England* (London: A. Crooke, 1669), p. 14; Blackstone, *Commentaries*, IV, 324.

56. *Laws of Maryland*, Feb. 1777, chap. 20; Iredell, *Laws of North Carolina*, pp. 284–86.

57. *Perpetual Laws of the Commonwealth of Massachusetts*, pp. 357–62; Metcalf, *Laws of New Hampshire*, IV, 71–74.

58. *Ibid.; Perpetual Laws of the Commonwealth of Massachusetts*, pp. 357–62; Mitchell and Flanders, *Statutes at Large of Pennsylvania*, IX, 45–47; see below, chapter 5.

59. Metcalf, *Laws of New Hampshire*, IV, 128–30; *Perpetual Laws of the Commonwealth of Massachusetts*, pp. 357–62; see also, Iredell, *Laws of North Carolina*, pp. 284–86.

60. Foster, *Crown Law*, 232–40.

61. Blackstone, *Commentaries*, IV, 358.

62. Mitchell and Flanders, *Statutes at Large of Pennsylvania*, IX, 45–47; Wilson, *Acts of the New Jersey Council and General Assembly*, pp. 4–5; Hening, *Statutes of Virginia*, IX, 168; *Laws of Maryland*, Oct. 1777, chap. 20, sec. 29; *Laws of the State of New York*, I, 173–84; *Perpetual Laws of the Commonwealth of Massachusetts*, pp. 357–62.

63. Blackstone, *Commentaries*, IV, 388.

64. Mitchell and Flanders, *Statutes at Large of Pennsylvania*, IX, 18–19, 45–47; Iredell, *Laws of North Carolina*, pp. 284–86; Hening, *Statutes of Virginia*, IX, 168; Wilson, *Acts of the Council and General Assembly of New Jersey*, p. 4; *Perpetual Laws of the Commonwealth of Massachusetts*, pp. 357–62.

65. Blackstone, *Commentaries*, IV, 92–93.

66. *Laws of the State of New York*, I, 43–44.

CHAPTER 4

1. Epaphroditus Peck, *The Loyalists of Connecticut* (New Haven, Conn.: Yale University Press, 1934), pp. 22–27; *The Independent Chronicle and Universal Advertiser* (Boston), March 20 and 27, 1777.

2. *Ibid.*

Notes

3. *Ibid.*
4. *The New York Gazette and The Weekly Mercury,* May 19, 1777.
5. Nathaniel Bouton (ed.), *Documents and Records Relating to the State of New Hampshire during the period of the American Revolution, from 1776 to 1783* (Concord, N.H.: E. A. Jenks, 1874), VIII, 324–31, 413–14, 416, 436, 568, 577, 578, 585.
6. *The Virginia Gazette* (Williamsburg, Va.: Purdie), June 6, 1777.
7. John G. L. Clark, "The Famous Dr. Stearns," *Proceedings of the American Antiquarian Society,* N.S., XLV, 317–424.
8. Robert E. Moody, "Samuel Ely: Forerunner of Shays," *The New England Quarterly,* V, 105–34.
9. Fitzpatrick, *Writings of Washington,* VI, 347, 397–98; VII, 61–62; Leonard Lundin, *Cockpit of the Revolution: The War for Independence in New Jersey* (Princeton, N.J.: Princeton University Press, 1940), pp. 159–65.
10. Allan Nevins, *The American States During and After the Revolution* (New York: Macmillan Co., 1924), p. 303; Wilson, *Acts of the New Jersey Council and General Assembly,* p. 14.
11. The state does not have custody of the court records. The suggestion of Standing Advisory Master Sidney Goldman that the counties might hold the records proved fruitless.
12. At least 40 persons were committed between April, 1777 and October, 1778. *Minutes of the Council of Safety of New Jersey,* pp. 17, 24, 25, 26, 31, 41, 64, 113, 128, 146, 167, 169, 189, 204, 269, 272, 274, 277, 284, 285.
13. *Pennsylvania Evening Post* (Philadelphia), Dec. 9, 1778; *New Jersey Gazette* (Trenton), Jan. 14 and July 20, 1778.
14. *New Jersey Gazette* (Trenton), June 3, 1778.
15. *The Pennsylvania Packet,* Feb. 11, 1777.
16. Speech of Governor William Livingston, Feb. 25, 1777 at Haddonfield (MS in State Library, Trenton, N.J.).
17. Ford and Hunt, *Journals of the Continental Congress,* X, 381–82.
18. *New Jersey Gazette* (Trenton), June 3, 1778.
19. *Selections from the Correspondence of the Executive of New Jersey, from 1776 to 1786* (Newark, N.J.: Printed at the Newark Daily Advertiser office, 1848), p. 137.
20. Dorothy C. Barck (ed.), *Minutes of the Committee and of the First Commission for Detecting and Defeating Conspiracies in the State of New York, December 11, 1776–September 23, 1778;*

Notes

with Collateral Documents, to which is Added Minutes of the Council of Appointment of the State of New York, April 2, 1778–May 3, 1779 (2 vols.; New York: New York Historical Society, 1924–25), I, 1–9, 11, 12, 16, 26, 78, hereafter cited as Minutes of the Committee for Detecting Conspiracies. A few were sent into Pennsylvania; see Samuel Hazard et al. (eds.), Pennsylvania Archives (Philadelphia: Printed by J. Severns and Co., 1852–56; Harrisburg, 1874–19——), Ser. 1, V, 40, hereafter cited as Pennsylvania Archives.

21. Journals of . . . Provincial Congress . . . of New York, I, 856–57, 885, 898.

22. New York v. Simon Mabee.

23. New York v. John Williams.

24. New York v. Job Babcock.

25. New York v. Anthony Hill.

26. New York v. John Likely; New York v. Anthony Umans.

27. New York v. Jacob Rosa et al.

28. Journals of . . . Provincial Congress . . . of New York, I, 876.

29. Ibid., pp. 888–89, 890–91, 919–21.

30. New York v. James Heutson et al.

31. Colonial Records of Pennsylvania, XI, 325–28.

32. Ibid., pp. 342, 344–47, 352, 386; XII, 778; Hazard, Pennsylvania Archives, Ser. 1, V, 665–67; VI, 25, 36–38, 45–53.

33. Ibid., pp. 445, 458, 460, 487–88, 507, 542–43, 569, 715–16, 744, 750, 769–70; Colonial Records of Pennsylvania, IX, 201–15.

34. Mitchell and Flanders, Statutes at Large of Pennsylvania, IX, 201–15.

35. Ford and Hunt, Journals of the Continental Congress, IX, 784–85, 1068; X, 384.

36. Fitzpatrick, Writings of Washington, II, 14–15, 179, 243–44; Hazard, Pennsylvania Archives, Ser. 1, VI, 361, 379, 414–15, 579.

37. A List of those Tories who Took Part with Great Britain, In the Revolutionary War, and Were Attainted of High Treason, Commonly Called the Black List (New York: Privately reprinted by J. M. Bradstreet and Son, 1865).

38. Hazard, Pennsylvania Archives, Ser. 1, VI, 641.

39. Pennsylvania v. Samuel Lyons et al.

40. United States v. George Spangler; United States v. Frederick Verner.

41. William B. Reed (ed.), Life and Correspondence of

Joseph Reed (Philadelphia: Lindsay and Blakiston, 1847), II, 23–26. The controversy raged in the contemporary press. In the *Pennsylvania Gazette* of March 19, 1777, "Demophilus" defended the constitution. He ended with the biting *"Quere,* does the Treason law . . . begin to squeeze some good people who had rather have had other folks fight and pay for their security until doomsday. . . ."

42. J. Thomas Scharf and Thompson Westcott, *History of Philadelphia, 1609–1884* (Philadelphia: L. H. Everts, 1884), I, 387–88, 395; *Pennsylvania Evening Post,* Oct. 21, 1778.

43. The procedural and substantive aspects of these cases are discussed in chapter 5.

44. Pennsylvania v. Abraham Carlisle; Pennsylvania v. John Roberts.

45. Hazard, *Pennsylvania Archives,* Ser. 1, VII, 21–44, 53–58.

46. Scharf and Westcott, *History of Philadelphia,* I, 394, cf., W. B. Reed, *Life of Joseph Reed,* II, 30; Nevins, *American States during and After the Revolution,* p. 256.

47. Pennsylvania v. John Elwood; Pennsylvania v. George Hardy; Pennsylvania v. James Stevens; Pennsylvania v. William Cassedy alias "Thompson"; Pennsylvania v. Isaac Green the younger; Pennsylvania v. Ralph Morden.

48. William H. Browne *et al.* (eds.), *Archives of Maryland* (Baltimore, Md.: Maryland Historical Society, 1883–19———), VII, 79, 82–83, 96–97.

49. Maryland v. Hamilton Callilo.

50. Browne, *Archives of Maryland,* XVI, 256, 308.

51. *Ibid.,* pp. 463, 488.

52. *Ibid.,* pp. 504, 507; Gust Skordas, Assistant Archivist, Hall of Records, Annapolis, Md., to the author, Jan. 23, 1951.

53. Among them was the notorious James Chalmers who had recruited the Maryland Loyalist Regiment. Eastern Shore-General Court Criminal Prosecutions, 1778–82 (MS in the Hall of Records, Annapolis, Md.); Browne, *Archives of Maryland,* XXI, 486–87; *Calendar of Maryland State Papers, The Black Books* (Annapolis: Maryland Historical Society, 1943), p. 224.

54. Maryland v. Edward Sutton; Maryland v. John Tims.

55. Maryland v. John Caspar Frietschie *et al.*

56. William P. Palmer (ed.), *Calendar of Virginia State Papers and Other Manuscripts, 1652–1784, Preserved in the Capitol at Richmond* (Richmond, Va.: n.p., 1875–93), I, 534–35; II, 56, 57.

107, 134, 144, 207, 213, 470, 496–97, 509–10, 511, hereafter cited as *Calendar of Virginia State Papers.*

57. *Ibid.,* p. 207; Freeman H. Hart, *The Valley of Virginia in the American Revolution, 1763–1789* (Chapel Hill, N.C.: University of North Carolina Press, 1942), p. 112.

58. Palmer, *Calendar of Virginia State Papers,* II, 285.

59. Virginia v. John Claypole *et al.*

60. Palmer, *Calendar of Virginia State Papers,* II, 183.

61. Virginia v. John Lyon; Virginia v. Will, a mulatto slave.

62. Virginia v. Fauntleroy Dye.

63. Palmer, *Calendar of Virginia State Papers,* III, 15, 101.

64. *Ibid.,* II, 626.

65. *Ibid.,* III, 120, 194, 361; the records of the general court for this period were destroyed by fire in April, 1865.

66. Hening, *Statutes of Virginia,* XI, 21–22, 129, 152, 253.

67. Josiah Phillips, though attainted as a traitor, suffered death under a court sentence for felony and robbery.

CHAPTER 5

1. Claude H. Van Tyne, *The Loyalists in the American Revolution* (New York: Macmillan Co., 1902), pp. xi, xii and chapters IX, X, XII. Note the choice of chapter titles. Alexander C. Flick, *Loyalism in New York during the American Revolution* (New York: Columbia University Press, 1901), p. 127; James W. Thompson, "Anti-Loyalist Legislation during the American Revolution," *Illinois Law Review* (1908), III, 81–90, 147–71.

2. *Selections from the Correspondence of the New Jersey Executive, from 1776–1786* (Newark, N.J.: Printed at the *Newark Daily Advertiser* office, 1848), pp. 63–67.

3. William H. Browne *et al.* (eds.), *Archives of Maryland* (62 vols.; Baltimore, Md.: Maryland Historical Society, 1883–19——), XVI, 488.

4. Hazard, *Pennsylvania Archives,* Ser. 1, VI, 744, 750, 769–70.

5. *Ibid.,* pp. 715–16.

6. *Journals of . . . Provincial Congress . . . of New York,* I, 856–57.

7. *Calendar of New York Historical Manuscripts, Relating to the War of The Revolution, in the Office of the Secretary of State, Albany, N.Y.* (2 vols.; Albany, N.Y.: n.p. 1868), II, 182.

8. *Journals of . . . Provincial Congress . . . of New York,* I, 902–5, 916, 926, 928, 965, 974, 975; New York v. Edward Palmer; cf., Flick, *Loyalism,* p. 127. Flick creates an inaccurate picture. "Imprisonment, branding on the hand, and fines ranging from $15 to $100 were common forms of punishment, and they were usually approved by the legislative power." In fact, no one was branded in New York. See the disallowance in *Journals of . . . Provincial Congress . . . of New York,* I, 970, 971.

9. Hazard, *Pennsylvania Archives,* Ser. 1, VI, 53, 361, 379, 414, 446–47, 579; *Calendar of New York Historical Manuscripts,* II, 83–85, 113, 115; Barck, *Minutes of the Committee for Detecting Conspiracies,* p. 25; Palmer, *Calendar of Virginia State Papers,* II, 163–64; Browne, *Archives of Maryland,* XLV, 482; *Minutes of the Council of Safety of New Jersey,* p. 18.

10. *Ibid.,* pp. 14, 186; *Journals of . . . Provincial Congress . . . of New York,* I, 1056; II, 272; Palmer, *Calendar of Virginia State Papers,* II, 40; *Colonial Records of Pennsylvania,* XI, 342; Barck, *Minutes of the Committee for Detecting Conspiracies,* pp. 30–31; Browne, *Archives of Maryland,* XXI, 29, 122, 481, 486–87.

11. *Ibid.,* pp. 29, 122; XLV, 467, 469; *Journals of . . . Provincial Congress . . . of New York,* I, 591; Palmer, *Calendar of Virginia State Papers,* II, 40; *Colonial Records of Pennsylvania,* XI, 342.

12. *Ibid.,* p. 43; XII, 553; Browne, *Archives of Maryland,* XVI, 535–36; XXI, 160; *Minutes of the Council of Safety of New Jersey,* pp. 12, 24, 25, 26, 31, 41, 53, 55, 64, 65, 82, 113, 128, 146, 167, 169, 189, 204, 269, 272, 277, 285; *Colonial Records of Pennsylvania,* XI, 43; XII, 553; Palmer, *Calendar of Virginia State Papers,* II, 207, 406; III, 419; *Correspondence of the New Jersey Executive,* pp. 107–8; *Calendar of Maryland State Papers, The Black Books,* p. 222; Barck, *Minutes of the Committee for Detecting Conspiracies,* II, 25, 57, 78, 139–40, 160–61, 179, 198, 209; *Journals of . . . Provincial Congress . . . of New York,* I, 1056; II, 272.

13. *Journals of . . . Provincial Congress . . . of New York,* I, 1104; *Minutes of the Council of Safety of New Jersey,* pp. 38, 58–59, 176; *Colonial Records of Pennsylvania,* XI, 565; XII, 401; Palmer, *Calendar of Virginia State Papers,* II, 163–64, 551; Browne, *Archives of Maryland,* XXI, 160, 486; *The Virginia Gazette* (Dixon and Hunter), Oct. 16, 1779; Eastern Shore-General Court Criminal Prosecutions, 1778–82 (MS in the Hall of Records, Annapolis, Md.).

14. Pennsylvania v. Joseph Griswold; *The New York Gazette*

and The Weekly Mercury, Sept. 7, 1778; *Minutes of the Council of Safety of New Jersey*, pp. 245, 270; Browne, *Archives of Maryland*, XVI, 155–56.

15. Pennsylvania v. Joseph Griswold.

16. Henry P. Johnston (ed.), *The Correspondence and Public Papers of John Jay* (New York: G. P. Putnam's Sons, 1890–93), I, 164.

17. *Pennsylvania Evening Post*, Oct. 21, 1778.

18. *Correspondence of the New Jersey Executive*, pp. 135–38; Hazard, *Pennsylvania Archives*, Ser. 1, VII, 59–60; Maryland v. Levin Disharoon; 1 Dallas 35.

19. Pennsylvania v. Abraham Carlisle; Hazard, *Pennsylvania Archives*, Ser. 1, VII, 44–45.

20. Pennsylvania v. Abraham Carlisle.

21. Opinion of Thomas McKean on the law of treason, June 23, 1777 (MS in the New York Public Library), cf., Blackstone, *Commentaries*, IV, 319.

22. With the exception of the New York courts-martial described in chapter 4.

23. Pennsylvania v. Abraham Carlisle. There is no evidence bearing on the two-witness requirement. It is probable that two witnesses to the *same* overt act were not required. The English rule permitted two witnesses to two acts of the same species of treason. 7 William III, c. 3; King v. Lowick; Hazard, *Pennsylvania Archives*, Ser. 1, VII, 44–48.

24. Pennsylvania v. John Roberts.

25. Pennsylvania v. Joseph Malin.

26. Successfully in Connecticut v. Gurdon Whitman, and in Virginia v. Thomas Davis.

27. Pennsylvania v. Abraham Carlisle.

28. Pennsylvania v. John Roberts.

29. *The Pennsylvania Evening Post*, Nov. 6, 1778.

30. Palmer, *Calendar of Virginia State Papers*, II, 169–70, 174, 305–6; *Calendar of New York Historical Manuscripts*, II, 179–82, 196–231.

31. Bernard C. Steiner, *Western Maryland in the Revolution* (Baltimore, Md.: The Johns Hopkins Press, 1902), p. 55; J. Thomas Scharf, *History of Maryland from the Earliest Period to the Present Day* (3 vols.; Baltimore, Md.: John B. Piet, 1879), II, 387; Dorothy M. Quynn, "The Loyalist Plot in Frederick," *Maryland Historical Magazine*, XL (1945), 201–10. In Maryland v. John Tims, the court gave the old common law sentence. It is doubtful

if the sentence was executed (Eastern Shore-General Court Criminal Prosecutions, 1778–81 [MS in the Hall of Records, Annapolis, Md.]).

32. Palmer, *Calendar of Virginia State Papers*, II, 285; *Journals of . . . Provincial Congress . . . of New York*, II, 470; *Calendar of New York Historical Manuscripts*, II, 125.

33. *Colonial Records of Pennsylvania*, XII, 222, 309, 778.

34. *Pennsylvania Packet*, May 4, 1779; *Journals of . . . Provincial Congress . . . of New York*, I, 814–904.

35. *Ibid.*, pp. 920–21, 976, 1039–40; Palmer, *Calendar of Virginia State Papers*, I, 590; II, 262, 624–25; Browne, *Archives of Maryland*, XVI, 157–58, 179; Ford and Hunt, *Journals of the Continental Congress*, IX, 1012; X, 381–82; *New Jersey Gazette*, June 3, 1778; Julian P. Boyd (ed.), *The Papers of Thomas Jefferson* (Princeton, N.J.: Princeton University Press, 1950——), II, 178–79.

36. Edward Coke, *The Third Part of the Institutes of the Laws of England*, pp. 4–5; Matthew Hale, *Historia Placitorum Coronae, The History of the Pleas of the Crown* (London: In the Savoy, 1736), I, 58–61, hereafter cited as *Pleas of the Crown;* Foster, *Crown Law*, pp. 183–86.

37. Barck, *Minutes of the Committee for Detecting Conspiracies*, p. 149.

38. *Ibid.*

39. The evidence is largely negative, i.e., there were no treason prosecutions in the period mentioned. See also, Pennsylvania v. Samuel Chapman; *Maryland Gazette*, Feb. 18, 1780; *Minutes of the Council of Safety of New Jersey*, p. 167; *Colonial Records of Pennsylvania*, XII, 71; Hazard, *Pennsylvania Archives*, Ser. 1, VII, 644–46.

40. Pennsylvania v. Samuel Chapman.

41. Hazard, *Pennsylvania Archives*, Ser. 1, VII, 644–46.

42. Hale, *Pleas of the Crown*, I, 165.

43. Pennsylvania v. Abraham Carlisle.

44. See a possible exception in *Minutes of the Council of Safety of New Jersey*, p. 204.

45. *Calendar of New York Historical Manuscripts*, II, 179–82, 165–68. A similar case in Pennsylvania that apparently was not regarded as treason is in Hazard, *Pennsylvania Archives*, Ser. 1, V, 665–66.

46. Cf., in Malin's case, the ruling that adherence to American troops was not treason whatever the intent.

47. *Minutes of the Council of Safety of New Jersey*, p. 275.
48. See chapter 4. The rising on the Eastern Shore of Maryland was another obvious example of levying war.
49. Foster, *Crown Law*, p. 218.
50. Pennsylvania v. Abraham Carlisle.
51. John Locke, *Two Treatises of Civil Government* (New York: E. P. Dutton and Co., 1924), p. 180.
52. Blackstone, *Commentaries*, IV, 319.
53. Delaware, New Jersey, and New York; Benjamin P. Poore (ed.), *The Federal and State Constitutions, Colonial Charters and Other Organic Laws of the United States* (Washington, D.C.: Government Printing Office, 1878), pp. 277, 1313, 1337–38.
54. Mitchell and Flanders, *Pennsylvania Statutes at Large*, XI, 109–14; *Laws of Maryland*, Oct., 1777, chap. 20; *Perpetual Laws of Massachusetts*, pp. 257–362; Henry H. Metcalf, *et al.* (eds.), *Laws of New Hampshire, Including Public and Private Acts and Resolves and the Royal Commission and Instructions, with Historical and Descriptive Notes, and an Appendix* (10 vols.; Bristol, N.H.: N. H. Musgrove Printing House, Vols. 3, 4; 1904–22), IV, 71–74; Thomas Cooper (ed.), *The Statutes at Large of South Carolina* (Columbia, S.C.: A. S. Johnston, 1836–41), IV, 479.
55. Hening, *Statutes of Virginia*, X, 66–71; *Laws of Maryland*, Oct., 1780, chaps. 45, 51; John R. Bartlett (ed.), *Records of the Colony of Rhode Island and Providence Plantations in New England* (Providence, R.I.: A. C. Greene and Bros., 1856–65), VIII, 609–15.
56. At common law by inquest of office. The finding by a jury in such an inquest that a person was an alien caused the real estate to revert to the crown. Further, say the *Commentaries*, "Alien enemies have no rights, no privileges, unless by the King's special favor, during the time of a war." Blackstone, *Commentaries*, I, 372.
57. *Laws of the State of New York*, I, 173–84; *Laws of the State of Delaware*, II, 636–43; Iredell, *Laws of North Carolina*, p. 342; Charles J. Hoadly (ed.), *The Public Records of the State of Connecticut* (Hartford, Conn.: Lockwood and Brainard Co., 1894–1922), II, 9–12; Allen D. Candler (ed.), *The Colonial Records of the State of Georgia* (Atlanta, Ga.: C. P. Bird, 1904–16), XIX, 126–27.
58. Mitchell and Flanders, *Pennsylvania Statutes at Large*, IX, 201–5; Wilson, *Acts of the New Jersey Council and General As-*

sembly, pp. 67–68; Cooper, *Statutes at Large of South Carolina,* IV, 568–70.

59. See the statutes cited in notes 54, 55, 57, 58, above.

60. *The Black List!*

61. New York, Westchester County, Court of Oyer and Terminer, Depositions and Indictments against . . . persons who have adhered to the enemies (MS in the New York Public Library); New York State Loyalists (A List of Loyalists against whom judgments were given under the confiscation act. MS in the New York Public Library).

62. Eastern Shore-General Court Criminal Prosecutions, 1778–1782 (MS in the Hall of Records, Annapolis, Md.). Maryland v. John Sterling; Maryland v. James Chalmers.

63. Whitehead, *Archives of the State of New Jersey,* Ser. 2, II, 364, 385, 388, 400–1, 401–2, 434–35, 470–71, 496–97, 519–20, 529, 530, 534, 543–44, 545, 552, 568, 581, 582; III, 49, 89, 90, 98–99, 165, 372–73, 527, 529–30; IV, 87–89. Evidence of final judgment and sale are in *ibid.,* III, 46–48, 49, 62–64, 68, 81, 92–98, 99, 111–13, 114–15, 128–33, 179–80, 396–97, 435, 449–51, 487–88, 508, 525–27, 588–89; IV, 406–7.

64. Both types were known to English law. See John Hatsell, *Precedents of Proceedings in the House of Commons; under Separate Titles with Observations* (London: n.p., 1781), IV, 77–78, 217–25, 300–7.

65. Metcalf, *Laws of New Hampshire,* IV, 191; *The Acts and Resolves, Public and Private of the Province of Massachusetts Bay,* V, 966–67; *Laws of the State of New York,* I, 173–84.

66. Hening, *Statutes of Virginia,* IX, 463–64; *Laws of the State of Delaware,* III, 636–43; Mitchell and Flanders, *Statutes at Large of Pennsylvania,* IX, 201–15; Walter Clark (ed.), *State Records of North Carolina* (Winston and Goldsboro, N.C.: Nash Brothers, 1886–1907), XXIV, 123–24.

67. Blackstone, *Commentaries,* IV, 259.

68. Poore, *Federal and State Constitutions, Colonial Charters . . . ,* X, 958, 959.

69. *Ibid.,* p. 1339.

70. Hening, *Statutes of Virginia,* IX, 463–64; W. P. Trent, "The Case of Josiah Phillips," *American Historical Review,* I (1896), 444–54.

71. For a fully documented discussion of the bill see Bradley Chapin, "The Law of Treason during the American Revolution" (Ph.D. dissertation, Cornell University Library, 1952).

Notes

CHAPTER 6

1. Max Farrand (ed.), *The Records of the Federal Convention of 1787* (New Haven, Conn.: Yale University Press, 1911), II, 136; III, 614.
2. *Ibid.*, II, 182.
3. *Ibid.*, II, 345, 346, 347.
4. *Ibid.*, II, 347.
5. *Ibid.*, II, 346.
6. *Ibid.*, II, 349.
7. *Ibid.*, III, 223.
8. *Ibid.*, II, 345.
9. *Ibid.*, II, 345, 346, 347.
10. *Ibid.*, II, 347.
11. *Ibid.*, II, 348.
12. *Ibid.*, III, 223.
13. *The Federalist*, I, 240.
14. Farrand, *Records of the Federal Convention*, II, 626, 627, 636.
15. Richard Peters (ed.), *The Statutes at Large of the United States* (Washington, D.C.: Little, Brown and Co., 1824–19——), I, 112, 118–19.
16. Leland D. Baldwin, *Whiskey Rebels; the Story of a Frontier Uprising* (Pittsburgh, Pa.: University of Pittsburgh Press, 1939).
17. Henry C. Lodge (ed.), *The Works of Alexander Hamilton* (New York: G. P. Putnam and Sons, 1904), VI, 355.
18. Opinion of William Bradford on the Law of Treason (MS, Pennsylvania Historical Society).
19. Albert Gallatin Letters (MS, New York Historical Society).
20. Francis Wharton (ed.), *State Trials during the Administration of Washington and Adams* (Philadelphia: Carey and Hart, 1849), pp. 166–73; United States v. Stewart; United States v. Mitchell.
21. United States v. Porter.
22. United States v. Vigol.
23. United States v. Mitchell.
24. Gallatin Letters (MS, New York Historical Society); the idea was Brackenridge's.
25. *Ibid.*

26. Fitzpatrick, *Writings of Washington,* XXXIV, 390.
27. James M. Smith, *Freedom's Fetters, the Alien and Sedition Laws and American Civil Liberties* (Ithaca, N.Y.: Cornell University Press, 1956), pp. 107–8.
28. W. W. H. Davis, "The Fries Rebellion, 1798–1799," *Era,* XII, 175–80; John B. McMaster, *A History of the People of the United States* (New York: D. Appleton, 1883–1913), II, 434–39.
29. *Aurora* (Philadelphia), March 12, 1799.
30. Wharton, *State Trials,* p. 502.
31. *Ibid.,* pp. 458–59.
32. *Ibid.,* pp. 459–64.
33. *Ibid.,* pp. 479–80.
34. *Ibid.,* pp. 497–534.
35. *Ibid.,* p. 534.
36. *Ibid.,* pp. 539–48, 553–57, 565–77.
37. *Ibid.,* pp. 584–99.
38. *Ibid.,* pp. 598–609.
39. Samuel H. Smith (recorder), *Trial of Samuel Chase, an Associate Justice of the United States, Impeached by the House of Representatives, Before the Senate of the United States* (Washington, D.C.: Printed for Samuel H. Smith, 1805), pp. 25–49, 127–46.
40. Wharton, *State Trials,* pp. 624–29.
41. *Ibid.,* pp. 633–37.
42. *Ibid.,* pp. 637–41.
43. Charles F. Adams (ed.), *The Works of John Adams: with a Life of the Author* (Boston: C. C. Little and J. Brown, 1850–56), VIII, 643–44.
44. *Ibid.,* pp. 644–45.
45. *Ibid.,* p. 648.
46. *Ibid.,* pp. 649–50.
47. *Ibid.,* p. 653.
48. *Ibid.,* IX, 21–23.
49. *Ibid.,* pp. 59–60.
50. *Ibid.,* pp. 60–61.
51. *Aurora* (Philadelphia), May 22, 23, 1800; *Gazette of the United States* (Philadelphia), May 23, 1800.
52. *Letter from Alexander Hamilton concerning the Public Conduct and Character of John Adams* (New York: Printed for John Lang by George F. Hopkins, 1800), pp. 41–45.
53. Adams, *Works of Adams,* IX, 270.

Notes

CHAPTER 7

1. Thomas P. Abernethy, *The Burr Conspiracy* (New York: Oxford University Press, 1954); for an excellent penetration of an historiographical bog see, Julius W. Pratt, "Aaron Burr and the Historians," *New York History*, XXVI (1945), 447–70.

2. David Robertson (reporter), *The Trial of Aaron Burr for Treason* (New York: J. Cockroft and Co., 1875), I, 574–78.

3. James Richardson (ed.), *A Compilation of Messages and Papers of the Presidents* (Washington, D.C.: Government Printing Office, 1896–99), I, 406, 412–17; *Annals,* 9th Cong., 2d sess., pp. 334–35, 357–59.

4. Everett Brown (ed.), *William Plumer's Memorandum of Proceedings in the United States Senate, 1803–7* (New York: Macmillan Co., 1923), pp. 485–86, 590–91; Worthington C. Ford (ed.), *The Writings of John Quincy Adams* (New York: Macmillan Co., 1913–17), III, 158; *Annals,* 9th Cong., 2d sess., pp. 403–24.

5. Brown, *Plumer's Memorandum,* p. 596; 1 Cranch 374; Albert J. Beveridge, *The Life of John Marshall* (Boston: Houghton Mifflin Co., 1916–19), III, 374.

6. 4 Cranch 75 *et seq.*

7. 4 Cranch 115 *et seq.*

8. 4 Cranch 125–27.

9. Charles F. Adams (ed.), *Memoirs of John Quincy Adams, Comprising Portions of his Diary from 1795 to 1848* (Philadelphia: J. B. Lippincott and Co., 1874–77), I, 448, 457–59; Brown, *Plumer's Memorandum,* p. 619; *Annals,* 9th Cong., 2d sess., pp. 471, 506–76.

10. As Claude Bowers would have it in *Jefferson in Power, the Death Struggle of the Federalists* (Boston: Houghton Mifflin Co., 1936), pp. 402–3, 424.

11. Winfield Scott, *Memoirs of Lieut.-General Scott* (New York: Sheldon and Co., 1864), I, 13; Henry Washington (ed.), *The Writings of Thomas Jefferson: being his Autobiography, Correspondence, Reports, Messages, Addresses, and Other Writings, Official and Private* (New York: H. W. Derby, 1861), V, 78–79, 81, 87–88, 94–100, 102–4, 112, 174–75, 187–88, 190–92.

12. Scott, *Memoirs,* I, 12.

13. Robertson, *Trial of Burr,* I, 1–92.

14. Pierre M. Irving (ed.), *The Life and Letters of Washington Irving* (Philadelphia: J. B. Lippincott and Co., 1872), I, 191.

15. Robertson, *Trial of Burr,* I, 93–187; Washington, *Writings of Jefferson,* V, 97.

16. Robertson, *Trial of Burr,* I, 243–360.

17. *Ibid.,* pp. 387–90, 404–81.

18. *Ibid.,* pp. 481–508.

19. *Ibid.,* pp. 535–48.

20. *Ibid.,* pp. 548–53.

21. *Ibid.,* pp. 555–60.

22. *Ibid.,* pp. 561–71.

23. *Ibid.,* pp. 571–93.

24. *Ibid.,* p. 617; II, 16–17.

25. *Ibid.,* II, 17, 100–1.

26. *Ibid.,* I, 659–60.

27. *Ibid.,* I, 487–98; II, 131–46, 236.

28. *Ibid.,* I, 488–89; II, 61–62.

29. *Ibid.,* I, 610–15, 626. The apposite adjudicated cases were: the Case of Nicholas Throgmorton; the Case of Alice Lisle. The former example of judicial tyranny occurred in the reign of Mary, the latter signaled the beginning of Jeffreys' "bloody assize" after the collapse of Monmouth's rebellion.

30. *Ibid.,* I, 619–20.

31. *Ibid.,* I, 627–51; II, 313–20.

32. *Ibid.,* II, 42–47, 81–89, 283–86.

33. Julius Goebel, Jr., "The Common Law and the Constitution," in W. Melville Jones (ed.), *Chief Justice John Marshall, a Reappraisal* (Ithaca, N.Y.: Cornell University Press, 1956), pp. 101–213.

34. Robertson, *Trial of Burr,* II, 496–97.

35. *Ibid.,* pp. 503–21.

36. *Ibid.,* pp. 497–502.

37. *Ibid.,* pp. 510–11, 531–32.

38. *Ibid.,* p. 545.

39. *Ibid.,* pp. 534–36.

40. *Ibid.,* pp. 523–27.

41. John P. Kennedy (ed.), *Memoirs of the Life of William Wirt, Attorney General of the United States* (Philadelphia: Lea and Blanchard, 1849), I, 221.

42. Edward S. Corwin, *John Marshall and the Constitution; a Chronicle of the Supreme Court* (New Haven, Conn.: Yale Uni-

versity Press, 1919); and in this vein see Bowers, *Jefferson in Power,* p. 422.

43. Richardson, *Messages and Papers of the Presidents,* I, 429.
44. *Annals,* 10th Cong., 1st sess., pp. 21–22.
45. *Ibid.,* pp. 55, 62.
46. *Ibid.,* pp. 61, 114, 125.

Table of Cases

Table of Cases

King v. Nicholas Bayard (1702), *Calendar of State Papers, American and West Indies, 1702,* pp. 230–31, 235; Dewey, *Calendar of Council Minutes,* p. 163; "The Case of William Atwood," New York Historical Society, *Collections,* XIII, 11 ff.; Howell, *State Trials,* XIV, 477.

King v. John Binckson alias "Long Finn" (1669), Paltsits, *Minutes of the Executive Council of the Province of New York,* I, 311–22.

King v. Elisha Cole (1767), John Tabor Kempe Lawsuits.

King v. William Dyer (1682), O'Callaghan and Brodhead, *Documents . . . Colonial History . . . of New York,* III, 289, 302–8; "Proceedings of the General Court of Assize," New York Historical Society, *Collections,* XLV, 3–38.

King v. Jacob Leisler (1691), Edmund B. O'Callaghan (ed.), *The Documentary History of the State of New York* (4 vols.; Albany: Weed, Parsons and Co., 1849–51), II, 205–8, 211–12; Dewey, *Calendar of Council Minutes,* p. 63; "Documents Relative to the Administration of Leisler," New York Historical Society, *Collections,* I, 311–14, 317, 333, 336–65; Colonial Entry Book, Ser. 5, Vol. MXXXVII, folios 7, 11, 13, 14, Colonial Office Papers; *Calendar of State Papers, America and West Indies, 1689–1692,* pp. 433, 671, 695; *1693–1696,* pp. 148, 231, 267, 470–71, 671; O'Callaghan and Brodhead, *Documents Relative to the Colonial History of New York,* III, *passim.*

King v. Jacob Milborne (1691), same sources as Leisler's case.

King v. William Prendergast (1765), Notes on the July Assize; *New York Gazette, or, the Weekly Post-Boy,* Sept. 1, 1766.

King v. Francis Rumbouts (1682), "Proceedings of the General Court of Assize" (MS in the New York Historical Society), pp. 3–38.

New York v. Job Babcock (1777), *Calendar of Historical Manuscripts Relating to the War of the Revolution in the Office of the Secretary of State,* II, 86–88.

New York v. James Huetson, Arnout Viele, *et al.* (1777), *ibid.,* pp. 196–231.

New York v. Anthony Hill (1777), *ibid.,* pp. 86–88.

New York v. John Likely (1777), *ibid.,* pp. 179–82.

New York v. Simon Mabee (1777), *ibid.,* pp. 83–85.

Table of Cases

New York v. Jacobus Rosa, Jacob Middagh, *et al.* (1777), *ibid.*,
pp. 113–15, 123–29; *Journals of . . . Provincial Congress
. . . of New York*, I, 889.

New York v. Anthony Umans (1777), *Calendar of Historical
Manuscripts*, II, 179–82.

New York v. John Williams (1777), *ibid.*, pp. 85–86.

PENNSYLVANIA CASES

Pennsylvania v. Abraham Carlisle (1778), 1 Dallas 40; Hazard,
Pennsylvania Archives, Ser. 1, VII, 44–52; *Colonial Records of
Pennsylvania*, XI, 606–7, 613, 614.

Pennsylvania v. Samuel Chapman (1781), 1 Dallas 53.

Pennsylvania v. William Cassedy alias "Thompson" (1779), *Colonial Records of Pennsylvania*, XII, 222–23, 309.

Pennsylvania v. George Cook, Jr. (1778), *Pennsylvania Evening
Post*, Oct 9, 1778.

Pennsylvania v. Peter Deshong (1778), *ibid.; Pennsylvania Archives*, Ser. 1, VI, 641

Pennsylvania v. John Elwood (1778), *ibid.*, Ser. 1, VII, 59–61;
Pennsylvania Evening Post, Nov. 6, 1778; *Colonial Records of
Pennsylvania*, XI, 624; XII, 48.

Pennsylvania v. Isaac Green the Younger (1781), *Colonial Records
of Pennsylvania*, XII, 778.

Pennsylvania v. Joseph Griswold (1780), *ibid.*, pp. 7, 85, 566;
Hazard, *Pennsylvania Archives*, Ser. 1, VIII, 649–52.

Pennsylvania v. William Hamilton (1778), *Pennsylvania Evening
Post*, Oct. 16, 1778.

Pennsylvania v. George Hardy (1779), *Colonial Records of Pennsylvania*, XI, 753–54, 761, 764; Hazard, *Pennsylvania Archives*,
Ser. 1, VII, 326–27; *Pennsylvania Packet*, May 4, 1779.

Pennsylvania v. Samuel Lyons *et al.* (1778), *Pennsylvania Evening
Post*, Aug. 28, 1778; *Colonial Records of Pennsylvania*, XI, 566,
579; Hazard, *Pennsylvania Archives*, Ser. 1, VI, 697–99.

Pennsylvania v. Joseph Malin (1778), 1 Dallas 33.

Pennsylvania v. Jacob Meng (1778), *Pennsylvania Evening Post*,
Oct. 9, 1778.

Pennsylvania v. Joshua Molder *et al.* (1778), 1 Dallas 33.

Pennsylvania v. Ralph Morden (1780), *Colonial Records of Pennsylvania*, XII, 535, 549; John M. Coleman, "The Treason of
Ralph Morden and Robert Land," *Pennsylvania Magazine of
History and Biography*, LXXIX (1955), 439–51.

Table of Cases

Pennsylvania v. John Roberts (1778), 1 Dallas 39; *Pennsylvania Evening Post,* Nov. 6, 1778.
Pennsylvania v. James Stevens (1779), Docket Book of Edward Shippen, Historical Society of Pennsylvania.
Pennsylvania v. John Taylor (1778), 1 Dallas 33.
Pennsylvania v. Joseph Turner (1778), *Pennsylvania Evening Post,* Oct. 21, 1778.
Case of Frederick Verner (1778), Hazard, *Pennsylvania Archives,* Ser. 1, VI, 697–99, 704, 713; VII, 246; Ford and Hunt, *Journals of the Continental Congress,* XI, 797–98; *Colonial Records of Pennsylvania,* XI, 561.

UNITED STATES CASES

Ex parte Bollman (1807), 4 Cranch 75.
United States v. Aaron Burr (1807), Robertson, *Trial of Aaron Burr.*
United States v. John Fries (1799), 3 Dallas 515; Wharton, *State Trials,* pp. 624–41; Smith, *Trial of Samuel Chase, passim.*
United States v. John Mitchell (1795), Wharton, *State Trials,* pp. 166–73.
United States v. George Spangler (1778), *Pennsylvania Magazine of History and Biography,* LV (1931), 49.
Ex parte Swartout (1807), 4 Cranch 75.
United States v. Frederick Verner (1778–79), *Colonial Records of Pennsylvania,* XI, 561; Hazard, *Pennsylvania Archives,* Ser. 1, VI, 704, 713; *Journals of the Continental Congress,* XI, 797–98.
United States v. Philip Vigol (1795), Wharton, *State Trials,* p. 166.

VIRGINIA CASES

In re Beverly (1682), Hening, *Statutes of Virginia,* III, 541.
King v. Sommersett Davies *et al.* (1683), *Virginia Magazine of History and Biography,* III (1896), 225–38; XVIII (1910), 253, 254.
King v. John Gunter and nine others (1663), *ibid.,* XV (1907–8), 38–43.
King v. Richard Lawrence (1685), *ibid.,* XI (1903–4), 63–64.
King v. Thomas Young and eleven others (1676–77), Hening, *Statutes of Virginia,* II, 545–48.
King v. Giles Bland and eight others (1676–77), *ibid.,* pp. 549–53; *Calendar of State Papers, America and West Indies, 1675–1676,* pp. 448, 493, 515; *1677–1680,* pp. 37, 40–42.

Table of Cases

Virginia v. James Caton *et al.* (1782), *Calendar of Virginia State Papers*, III, 194.

Virginia v. John Claypole *et al.* (1781), *ibid.*, II, 40, 164–65, 177, 207, 215–16, 683.

Virginia v. Thomas Davis (1777), *Virginia Gazette* (Purdie), Aug. 8, 1777.

Virginia v. Fauntleroy Dye (1781), *Calendar of Virginia State Papers*, II, 145–46, 169–70, 190.

Virginia v. John Gammon *et al.* (1781), *ibid.*, p. 626.

Virginia v. Albridgton Holland *et al.* (1782), *ibid.*, III, 361.

Virginia v. James Hughes (1782), *ibid.*, p. 120.

Virginia v. John Lyon (1781), *ibid.*, II, 305–6, 340, 350.

The Case of Josiah Phillips (1778), W. P. Trent, "The Case of Josiah Phillips," *American Historical Review*, I (1896), 444–54.

Virginia v. Robert Smith (1782), *Calendar of Virginia State Papers*, II, 624–25; III, 120.

Virginia v. Andrew Wayles *et al.* (1777), *Virginia Gazette* (Purdie), Aug. 8, 1777.

Virginia v. Will, a mulatto slave (1781), *Calendar of Virginia State Papers*, III, 90, 93.

MISCELLANEOUS CASES

Connecticut v. Moses Dunbar *et al.* (1777), *The Independent Chronicle and Universal Advertiser*, March 20, 1777.

Connecticut v. Elisha Wadsworth (1777), *ibid.*

Connecticut v. Gurdon Whitman (1777), *ibid.*

King v. Benjamin Merrill *et al.* (N.C., 1771), Saunders, *State Records of North Carolina*, VIII, 490, 495, 531–32, 635–36, 639, 643, 649–51.

Massachusetts v. Smith alias "Williamson" (1777), *Virginia Gazette* (Purdie), June 6, 1777; Samuel Stearns and John G. L. Clark, "The Famous Doctor Stearns," *Proceedings of the American Antiquarian Society*, N.S., XLV (1936), 317–424.

The Case of Asa Porter (N.H., 1776), Bouton, *Documents Relating to the State of New Hampshire*, VIII, 324–31, 413–16, 436, 568, 577, 578, 585.

Bibliography

PRIMARY SOURCES

Unpublished

Hall of Records (Annapolis)
Eastern Shore-General Court Criminal Prosecutions.

Library of Congress (Washington, D.C.)
The Washington Papers.

New Jersey State Library (Trenton)
Affirmation of Samuel Hugg.
Speech of Governor William Livingston, Feb. 25, 1777 at Haddon-field.

New York Historical Society (New York)
Albert Gallatin Letters.
John Tabor Kempe Lawsuits.
Notes on the July Assize.

New York Public Library (New York)
Miscellaneous Manuscripts. Opinion of Thomas W. McKean on the law of treason, June 23, 1777.
New York State Loyalists. A list of Loyalists against whom judgments were given under the confiscation act.
Westchester County, Court of Oyer and Terminer, Depositions and Indictments against persons who have adhered to the enemies of the state.

New York State Library (Albany)
Minutes of the Governor and Council of New York.

Pennsylvania Historical Society (Philadelphia)
Opinion of William Bradford on the Law of Treason.
Thomas W. McKean Papers.

Public Record Office (London)
Colonial Office, class 5, America and West Indies, Vol. 1278, Board of Trade Proprieties.

Bibliography

Colonial Office, class 5, America and West Indies, Vol. 137, Colonial Entry Book, Colonial Office Papers.

Colonial Office, class 5, America and West Indies, Vols. 159, 160, Correspondence of the secretary of state for the colonies with the attorney and solicitor general, 1772–81.

Published

Acts of the Privy Council of England, 1613–1783. 6 vols. Hereford: Great Britain, 1908–12.

Adams, Charles F. (ed.). *Memoirs of John Quincy Adams, Comprising Portions of his Diary from 1795 to 1848.* 12 vols. Philadelphia: J. B. Lippincott and Co., 1874–77.

———. *The Works of John Adams: with a Life of the Author.* 10 vols. Boston: C. C. Little and J. Brown, 1850–56.

Allen, Ethan. *A Narrative of Colonel Ethan Allen's Captivity, from the Time of his being Taken by the British, near Montreal, on the 25th day of September, in the Year 1775, to the Time of his Exchange, on the 6th Day of May, 1778.* Philadelphia: Printed for the author, 1799.

Annual Register, a Review of Public Events at Home and Abroad, The. London: Printed for J. Dodsley, 1758–19———.

Barck, Dorothy C. (ed.). *Minutes of the Committee and of the First Commission for Detecting and Defeating Conspiracies in the State of New York, December 11, 1776–September 23, 1778; with Collateral Documents, to which is added Minutes of the Council of Appointment of the State of New York, April 2, 1778–May 3, 1779.* 2 vols. New York: New York Historical Society, 1924–25.

Bartlett, John R. (ed.). *Records of the Colony of Rhode Island and Providence Plantations in New England.* 10 vols. Providence, R.I.: A. C. Greene and Brothers, 1856–65.

Blackstone, William. *Commentaries on the Laws of England.* 4 vols. Oxford: The Clarendon Press, 1778.

Bouton, Nathaniel (ed.). *Documents and Records Relating to the Province of New Hampshire, 1623–1800.* 7 vols. Concord, N.H.: Published by authority of the Legislature, 1867–73.

———. *Documents and Records Relating to the State of New Hampshire during the Period of the American Revolution, from 1776 to 1783.* 30 vols. Concord, N.H.: E. A. Jenks, 1884–1941.

Bibliography

Boyd, Julian P. (ed.). *The Papers of Thomas Jefferson*. Princeton, N.J.: Princeton University Press, 1950–19———.

Bradford, Alden (ed.). *Speeches of the Governors of Massachusetts, from 1765 to 1775; and the Answers of the House of Representatives to the Same*. Boston: Russell and Gardner, 1818.

Brown, Everett (ed.). *William Plumer's Memorandum of Proceedings in the United States Senate, 1803–1807*. New York: Macmillan Co., 1923.

Browne, William H., *et al.* (eds.). *Archives of Maryland*. 62 vols. Baltimore, Md.: Maryland Historical Society, 1883–19———.

Burnett, Edmund C. (ed.). *Letters of Members of the Continental Congress*. 8 vols. Washington, D.C.: Carnegie Institution, 1921–36.

Candler, Allen D. (ed.). *The Colonial Records of the State of Georgia*. 26 vols. Atlanta, Ga.: C. P. Bird, 1904–16.

———. *The Revolutionary Records of the State of Georgia*. 3 vols. Atlanta, Ga.: Franklin-Turner Co., 1908.

Carter, Clarence E. (ed.). *The Correspondence of General Gage with the Secretaries of State, 1763–1775*. 2 vols. New Haven, Conn.: Yale University Press, 1931.

Channing, Edward (ed.). *The Barrington-Bernard Correspondence and Illustrative Matter 1760–1770 Drawn from the Papers of Sir Francis Bernard (Sometime Governor of Massachusetts-Bay)*. Cambridge, Mass.: Harvard University Press, 1912.

Clark, Walter (ed.). *State Records of North Carolina*. 34 vols. Winston and Goldsboro, N.C.: Nash Brothers, 1886–1907.

Cobbett, William (ed.). *Parliamentary History of England, from the Norman Conquest, in 1066 to the year 1803*. 36 vols. London: Longman's and Co., 1806–20. Cited as *Hansard,* after the name of the official printer of parliamentary proceedings.

Coke, Edward. *The Third Part of the Institutes of the Laws of England*. London: Printed for A. Crooke, 1669.

Connecticut. *Acts and Laws of His Majesties Colony of Connecticut in New England*. Hartford, Conn.: Reissued by Case, Lockwood and Brainard Co., 1901.

Cooper, Thomas (ed.). *The Statutes at Large of South Carolina*. 13 vols. Columbia, S.C.: A. S. Johnston, 1836–41.

Cranch, William (reporter). *Reports of Cases Argued and Adjudged in the Supreme Court of the United States, 1801–1815*. 9 vols. Washington, D.C.: n.p., 1804–17.

Cumming, Robert C. (ed.). *The Colonial Laws of New York*

from the Year 1664 to the Revolution. 5 vols. Albany, N.Y.: J. B. Lyon, 1894.

Cushing, Harry A. (ed.). *The Writings of Samuel Adams.* 5 vols. New York: G. P. Putnam's Sons, 1904–8.

Dallas, Alexander (reporter). *Reports of Cases ruled and Adjudged in the Several Courts of the United States, and of Pennsylvania, Held at the Seat of the Federal Government.* 4 vols. Philadelphia: P. H. Nicklin, 1798–1807.

Delaware. *Laws of the State of Delaware from the Fourteenth Day of October, One Thousand Seven Hundred, to the Eighteenth Day of August, One Thousand Seven Hundred and Ninety-Seven.* 4 vols. New Castle, Del.: Samuel and John Adams, 1797–1816.

Dewey, Melvil (ed.). *Calendar of Council Minutes, 1668–1783.* Albany, N.Y.: University of the State of New York, 1902.

Farrand, Max (ed.). *The Records of the Federal Convention of 1787.* 3 vols. New Haven, Conn.: Yale University Press, 1911.

Fitzpatrick, John C. (ed.). *The Writings of George Washington from the Original Manuscript Sources 1745–1799.* 39 vols. Washington, D.C.: Government Printing Office, 1931–44.

Force, Peter (ed.). *American Archives: Consisting of a Collection of Authentick Records, State Papers, Debates and Letters.* 9 vols. Washington, D.C.: M. St. Claire Clarke and Peter Force, Ser. 4, 1837–46; Ser. 5, 1848–53.

Ford, Worthington C., and Gaillard Hunt (eds.). *Journals of the Continental Congress.* 25 vols. Washington, D.C.: Government Printing Office, 1904–28.

Ford, Worthington C. (ed.). *The Writings of John Quincy Adams.* 7 vols. New York: Macmillan Co., 1913–17.

Fortescue, John W., and W. Noel Sainsbury (eds.). *Calendar of State Papers, Colonial Series, America and West Indies.* London: Longman and Co., 1860–19——.

Foster, Michael. *A Report of some Proceedings on the Commission for the Trial of the Rebels in the year 1746, in the county of Surry; and of other Crown Cases: to which is added Discourses upon a few Branches of the Crown Law.* London: Printed for E. and R. Brookes, 1792.

Hale, Matthew. *Historia Placitorum Coronae, The History of the Pleas of the Crown.* 2 vols. London: In the Savoy, 1736.

Hamilton, Alexander. *Letter from Alexander Hamilton, concerning the Public Conduct and Character of John Adams, esq.,*

President of the United States. New York: Printed for John Lang by George F. Hopkins, 1800.

Hatsell, John. *Precedents of Proceedings in the House of Commons; under Separate Titles with Observations.* 4 vols. London: n.p., 1781.

Hazard, Samuel, *et al.* (eds.). *Pennsylvania Archives.* Philadelphia: Printed by J. Severns and Co., 1852–56; Harrisburg, 1874–19——.

Hening, William W. (ed.). *The Statutes at Large, Being a Collection of all the Laws of Virginia from the First Session of the Legislature in the Year 1619.* Richmond, Va., New York, and Philadelphia: Samuel Pleasant, Franklin Press, J. and B. Cochran, George Cochran, Thomas Desilver, 1809–23.

Historical Manuscripts Commission (Great Britain). *The Manuscripts of the Earl of Dartmouth* (Eleventh report, Appendix, Part 5; Fourteenth report, Appendix, Part 10). London: Eyre and Spottiswoode, 1887–97.

———. *Report on the Manuscripts of the Marquis of Lothian.* London: Mackie and Co., 1901–14.

———. *Report on the Manuscripts of Mrs. Stopford-Sackville.* 2 vols. London: Mackie and Co., 1904–10.

———. *Report on Manuscripts in Various Collections.* London: Mackie and Co., 1909.

Hoadly, Charles J. (ed.). *Records of the Colony or Jurisdiction of New Haven.* 2 vols. Hartford, Conn.: Lockwood and Co., 1858.

———. *The Public Records of the State of Connecticut.* 15 vols. Hartford, Conn.: Lockwood and Brainard Co., 1894–1922.

Howell, Thomas B. (ed.). *A Complete Collection of State Trials and Proceedings for High Treason and other Crimes and Misdemeanors from the Earliest Period to the Present Time.* 34 vols. London: Longman, Hurst, Rees, Orme, Browne and Green, etc., 1809–28.

Hutchinson, Peter O. (ed.). *The Diary and Letters of his Excellency Thomas Hutchinson.* 2 vols. London: S. Low, Marston, Searle and Rivington, 1883–86.

Hutchinson, Thomas. *The History of Massachusetts Bay.* London: John Murray, 1828.

Iredell, James (ed.). *Laws of the State of North Carolina.* Edenton, N.C.: Hodge and Wills, 1799.

Irving, Pierre M. (ed.). *The Life and Letters of Washington Irving.* 3 vols. Philadelphia: J. B. Lippincott and Co., 1872.

Bibliography

Johnson, Samuel. *Taxation No Tyranny.* London: Printed for W. Strahan and T. Cadell, 1776.

Johnston, Henry P. (ed.). *Correspondence and Public Papers of John Jay, 1763–1829.* 4 vols. New York: G. P. Putnam's Sons, 1890–93.

Kennedy, John P. (ed.). *Memoirs of the Life of William Wirt, Attorney General of the United States.* 2 vols. Philadelphia: Lea and Blanchard, 1849.

Laurens, Henry. *A Narrative of the Capture of Henry Laurens, of his Confinement in the Tower of London &C. 1780, 1781, 1782* (Collections of the South Carolina Historical Society, Vol. 1), Charleston, S.C.: S. B. Courtenay and Co., 1857.

List of those Tories who took part with Great-Britain, and were attainted of High Treason, commonly called the Black List, A. New York: privately reprinted by J. M. Bradstreet and Son, 1865.

Locke, John. *Of Civil Government, Two Treatises.* New York: E. P. Dutton and Co., 1924.

Lodge, Henry C. (ed.). *The Works of Alexander Hamilton.* 12 vols. New York: G. P. Putnam and Sons, 1904.

Maryland. *Calendar of State Papers, The Black Books.* Annapolis, Md.: Maryland Historical Society, 1943.

————. *Laws of Maryland, Made Since M, DCC, LXIII, Consisting of Acts of Assembly under the Proprietary Government, Resolves of the Convention, the Declaration of Rights, the Constitution and Form of Government, the Articles of Confederation, And, Acts of the Assembly Since the Revolution.* Annapolis, Md.: Frederick Green, 1787.

Massachusetts. *The Acts and Resolves, Public and Private, of the Province of Massachusetts Bay: to which are Prefixed the Charters of the Province.* 21 vols. Boston: Wright and Potter, 1869–1922.

————. *The Perpetual Laws of the Commonwealth of Massachusetts, from the Establishment of its Constitution to the First Session of the General Court in A.D. 1788.* Worcester, Mass.: Isaiah Thomas, 1788.

Massachusetts Historical Society. *Bowdoin and Temple Papers* (Collections, Ser. 6, Vol. IX). Boston: Massachusetts Historical Society, 1897.

————. *Warren-Adams Letters Being Chiefly a Correspondence among John Adams, Samuel Adams and James Warren* (Collections, Vol. LXXII). Boston: Massachusetts Historical Society, 1917.

Metcalf, Henry H., *et al.* (eds.). *Laws of New Hampshire, Including Public and Private Acts and Resolves and the Royal Commission and Instructions, with Historical and Descriptive Notes, and an Appendix.* 10 vols. Manchester: John B. Clarke and Co., Vol. 1; Concord, N.H.: N. H. Rumford Printing Co., Vols. 2, 5; Bristol, N.H.: N. H. Musgrove Printing House, Vols. 3, 4; Concord, N.H.: N. H. Evans Printing Co., Vols. 6–10, 1904–22.

Mitchell, James T., and Henry Flanders (eds.). *The Statutes at Large of Pennsylvania from 1682 to 1801.* 18 vols. Harrisburg, Pa.: C. M. Busch, 1896–1915.

Montesquieu, Charles Louis de Secondat, baron de la Brede. *The Spirit of Laws.* Worcester, Mass.: Isaiah Thomas, Jr., 1802.

Moore, Frank (ed.). *Diary of the American Revolution from Newspapers and Original Documents.* 2 vols. New York: Charles Scribner, 1860.

New Jersey. *Minutes of the Council of Safety of the State of New Jersey.* Jersey City, N.J.: J. H. Lyon, 1872.

―――. *Selections from the Correspondence of the Executive of New Jersey, from 1776 to 1786.* Newark, N.J.: printed at the *Newark Daily Advertiser* office, 1848.

New York. *Calendar of Historical Manuscripts, Relating to the War of the Revolution, in the office of the Secretary of State, Albany, N.Y.* 2 vols. Albany, N.Y.: n.p., 1868.

―――. *Journals of the Provincial Congress, Provincial Committee of Safety and Council of Safety of the State of New York, 1775–1777.* 2 vols. Albany, N.Y.: T. Weed, 1886–88.

―――. *Laws of the State of New York.* 5 vols. Albany, N.Y.: Weed, Parsons and Co., 1886–87.

O'Callaghan, Edmund B., and John R. Brodhead (eds.). *Documents Relative to the Colonial History of the State of New York.* 15 vols. Albany, N.Y.: Weed, Parsons and Co., 1853–87.

Palmer, William P. (ed.). *Calendar of Virginia State Papers and Other Manuscripts, 1652–1784, Preserved in the Capitol at Richmond.* 3 vols. Richmond, Va.: n.p., 1875–83.

Paltsits, Victor H. (ed.). *Minutes of the Commissioners for Detecting and Defeating Conspiracies in the State of New York, Albany County Sessions, 1778–1781.* 3 vols. Albany, N.Y.: J. B. Lyon Co., 1909–10.

Pennsylvania. *Colonial Records of Pennsylvania.* 16 vols. Philadelphia: n.p., 1852–53.

Bibliography

Peters, Richard (ed.). *The Statutes at Large of the United States.* Washington, D.C.: Little, Brown and Co., 1824–19———.

Pickering, Danby (ed.). *The Statutes at Large.* 24 vols. Cambridge, Eng.: n.p., 1762–1807.

Poore, Benjamin P. (ed.). *The Federal and State Constitutions, Colonial Charters and other Organic Laws of the United States.* 2 vols. Washington D.C.: Government Printing Office, 1878.

Reed, William B. (ed.). *Life and Correspondence of Joseph Reed.* 2 vols. Philadelphia: Lindsay and Blakiston, 1847.

Richardson, James (ed.). *A Compilation of Messages and Papers of the Presidents, 1789–1897.* 10 vols. Washington, D.C.: Government Printing Office, 1896–99.

Robertson, David (reporter). *Trial of Aaron Burr for Treason.* 2 vols. New York: J. Cockcroft and Co., 1875.

Saunders, W. L. (ed.). *Colonial Records of North Carolina (1662–1776).* 10 vols. Raleigh, N.C.: P. M. Hale, 1886–90.

Scott, E. H. (ed.). *The Federalist and other Constitutional Papers by Hamilton, Jay, Madison, and other Statesmen of their Time; with a full Index.* 2 vols. Chicago: Albert, Scott and Co., 1894.

Scott, Winfield. *Memoirs of Lieut.-General Scott.* 2 vols. New York: Sheldon and Co., 1864.

Scull, G. D. (ed.). *The Montresor Journals.* (New York Historical Society Collections for the Year 1881). New York: Printed for the New York Historical Society, 1881.

Seventy-Six Society. *Papers Relating to Public Events in Massachusetts Preceding the American Revolution.* Philadelphia: Printed for the Seventy-Six Society, 1856.

Smith, Samuel H. (recorder). *Trial of Samuel Chase, an Associate Justice of the United States, Impeached by the House of Representatives, before the Senate of the United States.* 2 vols. Washington, D.C.: Printed for Samuel H. Smith, 1805.

Smith, William J. (ed.). *The Grenville Papers: being the Correspondence of Richard Grenville Earl Temple K.G., and the Right Hon. George Grenville, their Friends and Contemporaries.* 4 vols. London: n.p., 1853.

Staples, William H. (ed.). *The Documentary History of the Destruction of the Gaspee.* Providence, R.I.: Knowles, Vose, and Anthony, 1845.

Stevens, Benjamin F. (ed.). *Facsimiles of Manuscripts in European Archives Relating to America 1778–1783.* 2107 facsimiles. London: Malby and Sons, 1889–95.

Bibliography

Taylor, William S., and John H. Pringle (eds.). *Correspondence of William Pitt.* 3 vols. London: John Murray, 1839–40.

Trumbull, J. Hammond, and Charles J. Hoadly (eds.). *The Public Records of the Colony of Connecticut.* 15 vols. A continuation, published uniformly with the above title, is entitled *The Public Records of the State of Connecticut.* 25 vols. Hartford, Conn.: Lockwood and Brainard Co., 1850–90.

United States. *Debates and Proceedings in the Congress of the United States, 1789–1825* (the *Annals*). 42 vols. Washington, D.C.: Gales and Seaton, 1849–56.

Washington, Henry (ed.). *The Writings of Thomas Jefferson: being his Autobiography, Correspondence, Reports, Messages, Addresses, and other Writings, Official and Private.* 9 vols. New York: H. W. Derby, 1861.

Wharton, Francis (ed.). *State Trials during the Administration of Washington and Adams.* Philadelphia: Carey and Hart, 1849.

Whitehead, W. A., et al. (eds.). *Documents relating to the Colonial, Revolutionary, and Post Revolutionary History of the State of New Jersey,* usually cited as *Archives of the State of New Jersey.* 42 vols. Newark, N.J.: Published by authority of the State of New Jersey, 1880–1949.

Wilson, Peter (ed.). *Acts of the Council and General Assembly of the State of New Jersey from the Establishment of the Present Government, and Declaration of Independence to the End of the First Sitting of the Eighth Session on the 24th Day of December, 1783.* Trenton, N.J.: Isaac Collins, 1784.

Newspapers

Aurora (Philadelphia).

Constitutional Gazette (New York).

Gazette of the United States (Philadelphia, New York).

Independent Chronicle and the Universal Advertiser, The (Boston).

New Jersey Gazette (Trenton).

New York Gazette and The Weekly Mercury, The (New York).

New York Post-Boy, The (New York).

Pennsylvania Evening Post (Philadelphia).

Pennsylvania Gazette (Philadelphia).

Pennsylvania Packet (Philadelphia, 1771–90).

Virginia Gazette, The (series published by Dixon and Hunter, and Purdie at Williamsburg).

Bibliography

SECONDARY SOURCES

Abbott, Wilbur C. *New York in the American Revolution.* New York: Charles Scribner's Sons, 1929.

Abernethy, Thomas P. *The Burr Conspiracy.* New York: Oxford University Press, 1954.

Alden, John R. *General Gage in America Being Principally A History of His Role in the American Revolution.* Baton Rouge, La.: Louisiana State University Press, 1948.

Arnold, Samuel G. *History of the State of Rhode Island and Providence Plantations.* 2 vols. New York: D. Appleton, 1859–60.

Baldwin, Leland D. *Whiskey Rebels; the Story of a Frontier Uprising.* Pittsburgh, Pa.: University of Pittsburgh Press, 1939.

Bancroft, George. *History of the United States from the Discovery of the American Continent.* 10 vols. Boston: Little, Brown and Co., 1834–75.

Beveridge, Albert J. *The Life of John Marshall.* 4 vols. Boston: Houghton Mifflin Co., 1916–19.

Bowers, Claude G. *Jefferson in power, the Death Struggle of the Federalists.* Boston: Houghton Mifflin Co., 1936.

Channing, Edward. *A History of the United States.* 6 vols. New York: Macmillan Co., 1905–25.

Clark, George N. *The Later Stuarts, 1660–1714.* Oxford: The Clarendon Press, 1934.

Clark, John G. L. "The Famous Dr. Stearns," *Proceedings of the American Antiquarian Society,* New Series, XLV (1934), 317–424.

Corwin, Edward S. *John Marshall and the Constitution; a Chronicle of the Supreme Court.* New Haven, Conn.: Yale University Press, 1919.

Davis, William W. H. "The Fries Rebellion, 1798–1799," *Era,* XII (1901), 175–80.

Flick, Alexander C. *Loyalism in New York during the American Revolution.* New York: Columbia University Press, 1901.

French, Allen. *General Gage's Informers, New Material Upon Lexington & Concord. Benjamin Thompson as Loyalist & the Treachery of Benjamin Church, Jr.* Ann Arbor, Mich.: University of Michigan Press, 1932.

French, Allen. *The First Year of the American Revolution.* Boston: Houghton Mifflin Co., 1934.

Goebel, Julius, and T. Raymond Naughton. *Law Enforcement in*

Bibliography

Colonial New York, a Study in Criminal Procedure, (1664–1776). New York: Commonwealth Fund, 1944.

Goebel, Julius. "The Common Law and the Constitution" in W. Melville Jones (ed.). *Chief Justice John Marshall, a Reappraisal*. Ithaca, N.Y.: Cornell University Press, 1956.

Hart, Freeman H. *The Valley of Virginia in The American Revolution 1763–1789*. Chapel Hill, N.C.: University of North Carolina Press, 1942.

Holdsworth, William S. *A History of English Law*. 12 vols. London: Methuen and Co. Ltd., 1931.

Hurst, Willard. "Treason in the United States," *Harvard Law Review*, LVIII (1944–45), 226–72, 395–444, 806–57.

————. *United States Supreme Court Briefs:* "Appendix to the Brief for the United States on Reargument," Anthony Cramer v. the United States, 325 U.S. 1.

Lundin, Leonard. *Cockpit of the Revolution: The War for Independence in New Jersey*. Princeton, N.J.: Princeton University Press, 1940.

McMaster, John B. *A History of the People of the United States from the Revolution to the Civil War*. 8 vols. New York: D. Appleton, 1883–1913.

Moody, Robert E. "Samuel Ely: Forerunner of Shays," *The New England Quarterly*," V (1932), 105–34.

Nettels, Curtis P. "A Link in the Chain of Events Leading to American Independence," *The William and Mary Quarterly*, Ser. 3, III, 36–47.

Nevins, Allan. *The American States During and After the Revolution, 1775–1789*. New York: Macmillan Co., 1924.

Pares, Richard. *War and Trade in the West Indies, 1739–1763*. Oxford: The Clarendon Press, 1936.

Peck, Epaphroditus. *The Loyalists of Connecticut*. New Haven, Conn.: Yale University Press, 1934.

Pratt, Julius W. "Aaron Burr and the Historians," *New York History*, XXVI (1945), 447–70.

Quynn, Dorothy M. "The Loyalist Plot in Frederick," *Maryland Historical Magazine*, XL (1945), 201–10.

Rowland, Kate M. *The Life of George Mason, 1725–1792*. 2 vols. New York: G. P. Putnam's Sons, 1892.

Scharf, J. Thomas. *History of Maryland from the Earliest Period to the Present Day*. 3 vols. Baltimore, Md.: John B. Piet, 1879.

Scharf, J. Thomas, and Thompson Westcott. *History of Philadelphia, 1609–1884*. 3 vols. Philadelphia: L. H. Everts, 1884.

Bibliography

Smith, James M. *Freedom's Fetters, the Alien and Sedition Laws and American Civil Liberties.* Ithaca, N.Y.: Cornell University Press, 1956.

Steiner, Bernard C. *Western Maryland in the Revolution.* Baltimore, Md.: The Johns Hopkins Press, 1902.

Thompson, James W. "Anti-Loyalist Legislation during the American Revolution," *Illinois Law Review,* III (1908–9), 81–90, 147–71.

Trent, W. P. "The Case of Josiah Phillips," *The American Historical Review,* I (1896), 444–54.

Van Tyne, Claude H. *The Loyalists in the American Revolution.* New York: Macmillan Co., 1902.

Wallace, David D. *The Life of Henry Laurens with a sketch of the Life of Lieutenant-Colonel John Laurens.* New York: G. P. Putnam's Sons, 1915.

Williams, Basil. *The Whig Supremacy, 1714–1760.* Oxford: The Clarendon Press, 1939.

Index

Index

Clinton, George, 52

Clinton, Sir Henry, 48, 58

Coke, Sir Edward, 9, 89, 108, 110

Colden, Cadwallader, 10–11

Commitment, process of, 65

Common law: as a source of state treason statutes, 39; received in state constitutions, 39; question of its relevance in federal courts, 107; John Marshall's knowledge of, 109; influence on colonial law of treason, 114; treason sentence given, 138–39n

Compassing the death of the king, 3; relationship to subversive words and conspiracy to levy war, 39

Confession: as evidence, 68

Confiscatory statutes: passed in Pennsylvania, 55; provisions in several states, 76–78

Congress, 83; defines procedure in treason cases, 84–85; debate on bill to suspend the writ of habeas corpus, 100–1; Jefferson asks for a review of Burr trial, 112

Connecticut: treason trial there, 46–47; confiscates Tory estates, 77

Conspiracy to levy war: relationship to compassing the death of the king, 40; treason in five states, 40, 89

Constitution: definition of treason, 81–83

Constructive treasons: origins, 3; use by Stuart judges, 4; in eighteenth century, 5; in the colonies, 7; Boston Tea Party as, 19; English doctrine accepted by several states, 40; Virginia draft riots as, 74; William Bradford's opinion, 85; applied to Whiskey rebels, 88–89; doctrine brought in by Federalist judges,

97; applied by counsel in the case of Bollman and Swartout, 101; not barred by John Marshall, 111

Continental Congress: unwilling to act against disaffected, 29; stiffens articles of war, 32–33; passes Tory Act, 34–35; passes treason resolutions, 36–37; recommendations concerning evidence, 43–44; recommends leniency in New Jersey, 49; assists Pennsylvania government, 54–55

Convention, Constitutional, 81–83

Cornwallis, Charles, Marquis, 27, 60, 61, 62

Corruption of the blood: a consequence of judgment, 8, 44; barred in several states, 44

Counsel, right to: guaranteed by several states, 43; available, 67

Court-martial: of Thomas Hickey, 35; trial of traitors by in New York, 51–54, 55, 64–65; in Pennsylvania, 56; trial of Nathaniel Bacon's adherents, 121n

Cranch, William, 101

Culpeper, Thomas, Lord, 7

Dallas, Alexander J., 93

Dartmouth, William Legge, Earl of, 17–18, 19, 21, 22

Declaratory Act, 11

Degrey, William, 13, 17

Delaware: authorizes use of English law, 39; confiscates Tory estates, 76–77

Denny, William, 19

Desertion: cases of, 56

Deshong, Peter, 56, 58

Dickinson, John, 12, 83

Duche, Jacob, 55

Dudingston, William, 16, 18

Dunbar, Moses, 46–47